Another Ray of
Sunshine
for the
Latter-day
Saint
Soul

Another Ray of Sunshine for the Latter-day Saint Soul

BOOKCRAFT

Salt Lake City, Utah

Library of Congress Catalog Card Number 99-76069
ISBN 1-57008-697-4

First Printing, 1999

Printed in the United States of America

Contents

The Workings of the Spirit

Faith and Prayer

The Power of the Word

Glimpses of Eternity

Missionary Work

Home and Family

On The Lighter Side

Preface

"There are occasionally hard days for each of us," President Gordon B. Hinckley stated. But he further counseled: "Do not despair. Do not give up. Look for the sunlight through the clouds" (*Teachings of Gordon B. Hinckley* [Salt Lake City: Deseret Book Co., 1997], p. 411).

In that spirit, *Another Ray of Sunshine for the Latter-day Saint Soul* offers readers 101 ways to "look for the sunlight."

With selections from such authors as Elaine Cannon, George D. Durrant, Randal A. Wright, Stephen R. Covey, Ardeth G. Kapp, Robert E. Wells, Hugh B. Brown, James E. Talmage, Spencer W. Kimball, and others, this compilation is designed to bring a ray of sunshine into all readers' lives. Embracing subjects from faith to forgiveness, service to sacrifice, hope to humility, these stories can lift, inspire, and help all who read them to look "through the clouds" and cultivate an attitude of happiness and a spirit of optimism.

Bookcraft expresses gratitude to the authors whose works are included in this publication. Thanks are also extended to Preston and Carrie Draper, Maureen Mills, Mindy Garff, and Lesley Taylor for their help in selecting, compiling, and arranging the stories and poems that make up this book.

It is the publisher's hope that readers will find *Another Ray of Sunshine* to be, in the tradition of other *Sunshine* books, inspiring, heartwarming, and soul-satisfying.

Love

Gifts of Love

ARDETH G. KAPP

It was Christmas Eve. The magic of Christmas seemed more real that year, not so much because of lights and tinsel, but because we had a feeling of excitement from the inside out. Family members had gathered at our house for our traditional dinner. Then Grandpa gathered us in the living room, opened the Bible, and read once again the Christmas story from Luke.

After the stockings were finally hung and treats left for Santa, the children reluctantly, yet eagerly, went to bed. They tried hard to get to sleep while listening intensely for any sounds from the expected night visitor.

"Now, if Heber would just go to bed, I could finish my gift for him," I said to myself. I had been working on this gift for my husband for about three months, and I needed about three more hours to complete it. But despite my encouragement for him to leave the room, he kept lingering. It was evident he would wait for me. I decided to go to bed and wait until he dropped off to sleep; then I'd slip out and finish his present.

With the lights out and the house quiet, I lay in bed looking into the dark, too excited to sleep. I listened for his heavy breathing, which would let me know it was safe to slip away. To my amazement, after a little while he whispered, "Ardie." I didn't respond. A conversation now would only delay the time when I could finish my project. To my great surprise, when I didn't answer he slipped out of bed as cautiously as I had planned to.

"What is he up to?" I wondered. I couldn't get up then. I waited and waited, but he didn't return. What should I do? Maybe if I went to sleep, I could awaken at about three o'clock and finish my project before everyone got up at about six, the time Grandpa Ted had agreed that we should all gather around the tree.

I was aroused from sleep when Heber got into bed ever so quietly. Only a few minutes later, his heavy breathing assured me he was sound asleep. It was three o'clock.

Months earlier, we had talked about Christmas and made the traditional gift list that ranged from the ridiculous to the sublime. At the top of my list was a wish that we could have more time together so he could teach me his great understanding of the gospel. I was driving two hours each day to BYU, and his schedule was very busy. Our time together was precious.

Heber's list of wants was short, as usual, but he did express a concern for the responsibility he had as a stake president to lead the way for his stake members, and it bothered him that his family history was not compiled. His family group sheets were incomplete.

My gift to him was finally wrapped. I could hardly believe I had done it, but there it was—the evidence of many hours of work. I hurried back and slipped into bed just in time to hear children's voices from the other room. "Grandpa says it's time to get up. Hurry! We can't wait!" they said. Neither could I.

In the living room Heber handed me a package. I opened it and found a box of cassette tapes. On top of the box was a message: "My dear Ardie, While you are traveling each day, I will be with you. As you know, the Doctrine and Covenants has been of special interest to me over the years. I have enjoyed reading and recording for you the entire book. Reading it with the purpose of sharing it with you, I have endeavored to express my interpretation and feelings so that you might feel what I feel about this sacred book. I finished it only a few hours ago. May these tapes add to your wisdom and help unfold the mysteries of God and prepare us for our eternal life together."

Then I handed Heber my gift. He tore off the wrapping, and inside was a book of remembrance—many pages of pictures and stories never before recorded, a result of secret trips to visit and interview relatives and the assembling of records and histories.

On the first page of the gift was a message: "Dear Heber, As I have copied, reviewed, and prepared these sheets and interviewed family members, your ancestors have become very real to me, and I have an increased appreciation and understanding of the greatness and nobility in the man I married. Although I never met your father, and met your mother only once, when I meet them I know I'll love them and know them better because of this gift I have prepared for you, which really has been a gift for me."

I don't remember any of the other gifts we received that year, but Heber and I will never forget the spirit of that glorious Christmas celebration.

The Yellow Dress

Janene Wolsey Baadsgaard

Growing up in the middle of eight girls, I rarely addressed my sisters by name. I called one sister "Leave my things alone," another, "It's your turn to do the dishes," and still another, "You always use all the hot water."

Being a sister in my house was not so much a choice as a fact. It was something I would have avoided at times. But there were other times . . . times like my graduation night.

Diane and Mary, my two older sisters, had tried for years to transform me. They were both great at applying makeup, styling hair, and selecting fashionable clothes. They had boyfriends, went to dances and parties, and spent hours sunbathing in the back-yard.

I was their embarrassing younger sister. I thought sunbathing was a fancy name for wasting a whole afternoon in the lounge chair sweating. Nylons made my legs itch and hair spray made the fuzzies in my nose stiff. Even when we were small children and played with paper dolls together, Diane and Mary were left with gaping mouths when I freed all my paper ladies from their glamorous, frozen poses. I regularly cut my paper dolls up to their navels so they could run.

It had been a valiant effort. These two older sisters had worked on me for eighteen years without much success.

Then came the early evening before my high school seminary graduation. I was downstairs in my bedroom looking through the closet for something nice to wear. On rare occasions I could be persuaded to take a bath and wear a dress. This was a rare occasion. I was going to be one of the speakers, and I wanted to look nice.

My closet was full of hand-me-downs from Diane and Mary. It had never bothered me until now. It was the end of the month, and the family paycheck hadn't been able to stretch quite far enough to include a new graduation dress for me.

I understood. Being raised in the middle of many children teaches one to understand a lot of things. But sometimes it doesn't take away the wishing. I was wishing I had a new dress to wear.

I selected a nice navy blue dress with a white lace collar and pearl buttons. It had been Mary's graduation dress two years ago and it would just have to do. I zipped up the dress and slipped on a pair of dressy black shoes. They were run over on the heel and fit the foot form of their previous owner, my older sister Diane. They would have to do, too.

I grabbed my speech and walked upstairs, ready to leave. When I got to the head of the stairs, I saw Diane and Mary standing together smiling. Each of them was holding a package wrapped with fancy paper and shiny bows like the expensive department stores used.

Most of our family presents were wrapped in paper and bows my mom had saved from previous birthdays and holidays. We were taught to unwrap carefully.

I took the presents from my sisters as they put their arms around me and kissed me on both cheeks. The first present was large and rectangular. I opened the gift slowly, being careful not to rip the fancy wrapping paper under the tape. When I lifted the lid and folded back the tissue paper, a bright yellow chiffon dress with folded pleats on the front yoke shone out with the same warmth as the smiles on my sisters' faces.

The next box held a pair of bright yellow shoes, an exact match, with round toes and ties. A middle child in a large family never gets a pair of bright yellow shoes. It's just not practical.

"Run downstairs and put them on," Diane said.

"Hurry, or you'll be late," Mary added.

I ran back downstairs and tried on my new outfit. As I slipped the dress over my head and tied the laces on the shoes, I was magically transformed. I felt beautiful.

Diane was at that time a newlywed struggling to pay a huge medical debt incurred with her first baby daughter, who had died of a heart defect. Mary was a college student working hard to earn her tuition. The money to buy that dress and shoes did not come easily, and I knew it.

When I stood up to give my speech that night, I was clothed in something more than new clothes. It wasn't so much the dress and shoes as it was the whole shared history before—midnight talks on the double bed, the letter tucked under my pillow after I lost the election, crowded bathrooms, and tied-up telephones.

We were sisters.

To This End

JOHN OXENHAM

And hast Thou help for such as me,
Sin-weary, stained, forlorn?
"Yea then,—if not for such as thee
To what end was I born?"

But I have strayed so far away,
So oft forgotten Thee.
"No smallest thing that thou hast done
But was all known to Me."

And I have followed other gods,
And brought Thy name to scorn.
"It was to win thee back from them
I wore the crown of thorn."

And, spite of all, Thou canst forgive,
And still attend my cry?
"Dear heart, for this end I did live,
To this end did I die."

And if I fall away again,
And bring Thy Love to shame?
"I'll find thee out where'er thou art,
And still thy love will claim."

All this for me, whose constant lack
Doth cause Thee constant pain?
"For this I lived, for this I died,
For this I live again."

$\mathscr{L}$earning About Love

GINA JOHNSON

I was five years old when I learned how cruel kids can be. My friend and I were riding the bus to school, and there was a little girl with blond hair sitting behind us. We didn't know her, but we knew her name was Sue.

As Sue sat there, my friend and I began to hurt her. We pushed her and scratched at her arm. We said mean things to her. Why? Had Sue done something to prompt this hurtful and cruel behavior? No. Her only "crime" was that she looked different. Her mouth was different from ours, and when she spoke, it sounded different. She sat silently and endured our cruelty. She could have called to the bus driver, or told us to stop . . . but she chose not to.

After arriving at school I was called to the principal's office. I can still remember the look on Mrs. Barto's face and the sadness in her eyes. She asked me why I had behaved the way I did toward Sue. I hung my head and said I didn't know, and I honestly didn't. That was the sad part. That was the last day Sue ever came to our school.

Years later in high school, I met Sue again. She was so nice to me. Though she didn't recognize me, I knew it was her. I could still see the mild trace of a scar on her upper lip. How I wanted to go to her and tell her how sorry I was that I had been a mean little kid! But instead I hid in the anonymity of being a teenager. She never knew it was me, and I never had the courage to tell her.

In a hospital room some twenty-six years after kindergarten, my fifth baby was born. The words they used to describe him were hard for me to hear: "Down's syndrome." How could my beautiful baby suddenly be so different, simply because of a name? Then I came across this poem:

If apples were pears
and peaches were plums
and the rose had a different name.

If tigers were bears
and fingers were thumbs
I'd love you just the same.

—Anonymous

As I looked at my newborn son, my heart ached. All I could think about was Sue. Had her mother held her and loved her, just as I did David? Of course she had. Though David looked different to the doctors, he looked beautiful to me. All of a sudden I realized that someday others might be as cruel to David as I had been to Sue. And all because he was different.

It felt as if my life was shattering. I felt like God had made a mistake in sending David to me. I was sure some other mother could love him more and be a better mom for him. I didn't think I had what it took to be the mom of a child with a disability. What a hard reality for me, to know that for the rest of his life David would be both mentally and physically handicapped. This was more than I could bear.

A phone call came to the hospital. It was my friend Kris Holladay. With her usual love and warmth she said, "I hear you have a beautiful baby boy!" My mind raced. Surely no one had told her about David because they didn't want to hurt her. One of Kris's children, Kari, was severely mentally and physically handicapped and wasn't expected to live very long.

I had never quite understood Kris. She treated Kari as you would any baby. She sincerely loved her and enjoyed every minute with her. I never once saw that look of disappointment that I thought the mother of a child with a severe disability should have. Secretly I sometimes wondered if she really understood how bad off Kari was. If she did, she surely wouldn't be so happy.

I didn't know the words to say, but I knew I had to tell her the truth. Through my tears I said, "I do, Kris, but he's handicapped."

With enthusiasm and love in her voice she replied, "I know. Isn't that wonderful?" I was so taken aback. When she said that to me it was almost as if she were sharing a delightful secret that only she and I knew.

At that moment, I knew Kris had lost her mind. How could she, of all people, be happy for me? Didn't she know that one of the first "rules" in the unwritten handbook for parents of kids with disabilities was that we are supposed to be depressed? But something in her voice gave me hope.

Yet, even with that hope, I struggled. I had never grieved so much for anything or anyone in my life as I did for my David. Then one night a dear friend, Toni Brown, suggested we go to the hospital to see him. As we drove we exchanged the usual small talk. Out of the blue Toni asked, "Gina, how are you doing?" I said, "Fine." With kindness in her eyes and a gentle voice she said, "No, I mean . . . how are you *really* doing?"

She caught me off guard, and before I could stop myself I was crying and telling her how I felt like my heart was breaking. With excitement in her voice she said, "Well, didn't you see *The Grinch Who Stole Christmas?*" I nodded my head, though I didn't understand what she meant. She told me that in the story, the Grinch's heart had to break before it could grow bigger and hold more love. She told me that was what was happening to me. Somehow I knew she was right.

Six years passed, and I met a wonderful young man named Daniel Hughes. He had Down's syndrome as well but was a lot further ahead than David. He was much like any other young man. He was polite and delightful to talk to. Daniel looked at David, and then back at his mom. With a question in his voice he said, "Mom . . . David has my face." Immediately I choked and my eyes began to sting from tears. I felt that old, familiar pain. If even Daniel could see the differences in David, there was no doubt that others would see them too.

I felt so sorry for his mom. I wondered what she could possibly say to him. I was humbled as I heard her reply: "Yes, Daniel . . . it's a sweet face, isn't it?"

I couldn't get over her words. As we walked to our separate

cars, I could hardly contain my emotions. Just then Daniel looked back and waved to us. As he did, he yelled, "Good-bye, handsome!"

Are there unkind children still left in this world? Perhaps. But my experience has been that most kids are good and kind. They all seem to have a wonderful blindness. They do not see all that is wrong with my son, only what is right.

How do I say thank you for being taught what really matters in life?

I have learned so many things as people have shared with me the gifts of the heart, even when I did not deserve them.

Sue taught me forgiveness. Kris taught me to be able to see what others could not see: the worth of a child. As I watched her love and serve Kari, she taught me how to love my son simply because he was my son—unconditionally, as Jesus would.

Kari and her family taught me what true "quality of life" is. I saw it as I watched Tricia, Kari's eight-year-old sister, tickle her, kiss her, and love her. And I saw it even more as Kari would giggle with delight at the love being showered upon her. As Kari's sweet Doctor Beyda so eloquently said after she died, "Quality of life is simply the ability to give or receive love."

I remember Kris told me that when Kari was born the doctors said she would live only a few days. So Kris made a list of things she wanted to do before her baby died. She wanted to kiss her, sing to her, rub baby lotion on her, put a pink bow in her hair, cut a locket of her hair, and tell her how much she loved her. Kris believed that each day after completing that list was a "bonus" day. Kris was given 3,779 bonus days.

Toni showed me how to find joy in a broken heart. Daniel helped me to see what is truly beautiful and handsome. David taught me that the only sadness I should feel at the birth of a child with a disability is for those who have not yet learned how to love him.

Most of all, how do I say thank you to a loving Father in Heaven who trusted me enough to give me David? For it is through David that I am learning how to be the person God intended all along.

13

"Jeff, I Love You"

MAX H. MOLGARD

Laura had been disturbed for a long time by the declared open war that was going on between her mother and her sixteen-year-old brother Jeff. As time had passed, things seemed to grow worse between Jeff and her mother. One of the main bones of contention was a garbage pit in the house called Jeff's bedroom.

Every day, each conversation between Jeff and his mother seemed to be centered around the bedroom. Jeff refused to do anything about the bedroom, and his mother said that she was not going to clean it for him. Jeff always said it was his room and he should be able to leave it dirty if that was what he chose to do. Then he'd ask his mom, "What is a little clutter going to hurt?"

His mom always countered with something like: "Don't you know that cleanliness is next to godliness?" Or, "How can you bring your friends into this mess?" Or, "What will the neighbors think?" And when those words didn't bring a response, she'd end with, "This is my house and I will not tolerate such a mess!" These conversations invariably ended with the volume being turned to the maximum and Jeff going to his bedroom and slamming the door behind him.

One day Laura came home and heard strange noises coming from Jeff's bedroom. It sounded as if someone was cleaning. She wondered if she was dreaming.

As she looked into the room, she saw her mother cleaning. She asked, "Mother, what in the world are you doing?"

Her mother smiled and answered simply, "Cleaning Jeff's bedroom." Laura was so stunned that she turned around and walked away.

Laura later started to doubt what she had seen; and wondering if it could really be true, she returned to Jeff's bedroom. Her mother was gone, but what she thought she had seen was true.

14

The bedroom was cleaner than it had been for months. As Laura stood looking around the room in amazement, she noticed a piece of paper lying on the bed. She thought her mother must have missed it. Picking up the paper, she found that it was a note from her mother. The note read: "Jeff, I love you! Mom."

When Jeff came home and found the note, a miracle took place. Things were never again the same between Jeff and his mother; the two seemed to get along better each day.

Shards of Good Intentions

H. Wallace Goddard

I remember a time in my life when I felt very discouraged and worthless. A dear friend named Jack Stone drove many miles and stayed up most of the night to talk with me. He told me a story about his young daughter, who, as her mother's birthday approached, wanted to give her mother a very special gift. But the little girl had no money and very limited, childish skills. So, at her father's prompting, she gathered up the most interesting things she could find, scraps of paper, bits of string, macaroni, watercolors, and glitter. She lovingly glued and painted her treasured finds to a piece of paper and wrapped her gift for her mother. On the appointed day she proudly presented the gift to her mother. What would you guess was the mother's reaction to the gift? Do you think she cringed at the needless waste of macaroni? Do you think she scoffed at the unskilled assembly? No. The mother knelt on the floor in front of her dear child, embraced her, and wept with joy. The mother was touched by the child's sweet message of devotion.

Perhaps it is the same when we make our gifts to Heavenly Father. They are nothing more than shards of good intentions and scraps of struggle. But he is pleased with our earnest effort, and he embraces us in his love.

Hi, Teacher!

SHELDON L. ANDERSON

You wonder why they greet her so?
Come watch her teach the three-year-olds.
She simplifies so they can learn,
But with it all, her heart enfolds.

Her heart enfolds, as do her arms,
To give each child a sense of worth.
She teaches color, shape, and sound,
And thankfulness for life on Earth.

They leave, and she stands at the door
To say farewell to every tot.
She hugs, and pats, and sends them forth,
"I'm glad you came," her parting thought.

You wonder why they run to her,
And why, years later, hug her tight?
With love, she nourishes their souls.
With love, she leads them in the light.

The Daily Portion of Love

H. Burke Peterson

Among the tragedies we see around us every day are the countless children and adults who are literally starving because they are not being fed a daily portion of love. We have in our midst thousands who would give anything to hear the words and feel the warmth of this expression. We have all seen the lonely and discouraged who have never been told.

A few years ago I was assigned to tour a mission in another land. Before our first meeting with the missionaries, I asked the mission president if there were any particular problems I needed to attend to. He told me of one missionary who had made up his mind to go home early—he was very unhappy. "Could I help him?" I asked. The president wasn't sure.

As I was shaking hands with the missionaries before the meeting, it wasn't hard to tell which one wanted to leave. I told the president if he didn't mind I'd like to speak to the young man after the meeting. As I watched him during the meeting, about all I could think of was the big piece of gum he had in his mouth. After the meeting this tall, young missionary came up to the stand.

"Could we visit?" I asked.

His response was an implication that he couldn't care less.

We went to the side of the chapel. We sat together as I gave him my very best speech on why missionaries should not go home early. He kept looking out of the window, paying absolutely no attention to me.

Off and on we were in meetings together for two days. One time he even sat on the front row and read the newspaper as I talked. I was baffled and unnerved by him. By now it appeared to me that he should go home—and soon! I'd been praying for a way to reach him for two days, but to no avail.

The last night after our meeting I was visiting with some folks in the front of the chapel. Out of the corner of my eye I saw the Elder. At that very moment I had a feeling about him enter my heart that I had not yet experienced. I excused myself, went over to him, took his hand, looked him in the eye, and said, "Elder, I'm glad I've become acquainted with you. I want you to know that I love you."

Nothing more was said as we separated. As I started out the chapel door for our car, there he stood again. I took his hand again, put my arm around him, looked up in his eyes and said, "What I said to you before, I really mean. I love you; please keep in touch with me."

Spirit communicates to spirit. It was then that his eyes filled with tears and this boy said simply, "Bishop Peterson, in all my life I can never remember being told 'I love you.'"

Now I knew why he was confused, disturbed, insecure, and wanted to leave the mission field.

In speaking of a son or daughter, some will say, "He ought to know I love him. Haven't I done everything for him? I buy him clothes, give him a warm home, an education, and so on." Make no false assumptions: unless the person feels that the need has been filled, the parent's responsibility has not been accomplished.

We must make an even clearer effort to communicate real love to a questioning child. The giving of love from a parent to a son or a daughter must not be dependent on his or her performance. Ofttimes those we think deserve our love the least need it the most.

$\mathscr{I}$t Didn't Hurt Anymore

H. WALLACE GODDARD

The first lesson from Father about love may be to make time. That may seem quite easy for an eternal being. We mortals must use our creativity to find time for our children.

I remember when Andy caught me one evening just as I was dashing off to a Church meeting. He told me that his leg hurt. It had hurt all day. He thought something might be very wrong with it. He wanted me to help him. I wanted to be a good dad, but I had to go to a meeting. I was tempted to dismiss his pain: "It'll get better. It's probably just growing pains. You'll be okay." I even thought about judging him: "Andy, don't complain so much. We took you to the doctor when you had chest pains, and it was nothing." But I knew those approaches would not help. I felt trapped. In desperation I suggested: "Andy, I am going to a meeting. It will not go late. May I pick you up after the meeting? We will go out for dessert and talk about it. Is that all right?" Andy readily agreed. So, after the meeting I dashed home and picked up Andy, and we went to a restaurant. We ate and played tic-tac-toe on the paper place mats. We talked. And his leg didn't hurt anymore.

Service AND *Sacrifice*

"Thank You for Letting Me Give to You"

HAROLD C. BROWN

My son was on a mission in Oaxaca, Mexico, where the Saints were very, very poor. Nevertheless, they fed the missionaries. Our son is six foot seven, and our food bill was cut in half when he left. It was cheaper to send him than to keep him home. He seemed to eat everything and anything. He and his companion were invited into the home of a woman he referred to as the poorest woman in the ward in Oaxaca. They sat down to a dinner of beans and tortillas. He wrote to us, "We ate it all." She asked if they would like more. As I was reading his letter, I thought, *Please, Troy, say no.* But he said, "Yes, please." So she served him the rest of the beans. Then she said, "I have one very small egg left. Would you like that?" Again, as a father I thought, *Please, say no.* But he said, "Yes, please." She fried the small egg and cut it in half for those two missionaries and fed them. Then they started to read the scriptures to express their gratitude for what she had done. She broke down in tears and said, "Thank you, thank you. I have felt that others who have come to my home did not like my food. Thank you for letting me give to you."

"Unto One of the Least of These"

SUSAN FARR-FAHNCKE

He was kind of scary. He sat there on the grass with his cardboard sign and his dog (actually his dog was adorable). Tattoos ran up and down both arms and even reached his neck. The sign proclaimed him to be "stuck and hungry" and asked for help.

A wimp for anyone needing help, I pulled the van over and in my rearview mirror contemplated this man, tattoos and all. He was youngish, maybe forty. He wore one of those bandannas tied over his head, biker-pirate style. Anyone could see that he was dirty and had a scraggly beard. But if you looked closer, you could see that he had neatly tucked in his black T-shirt and that his things were in a small, tidy bundle. Nobody was stopping for him. I could see the other drivers take one look and immediately focus on something else—anything else.

It was so hot out. I could see in the man's very blue eyes how dejected and tired and worn out he felt. The sweat was trickling down his face. As I sat with the air-conditioning blowing, the scripture suddenly popped into my head: "Inasmuch as ye have done it unto one of the least of these my brethren, ye have done it unto me" (Matthew 25:40).

I reached down into my purse and extracted a ten-dollar bill. My twelve-year-old son, Nick, knew right away what I was doing. "Can I take it to him, Mom?"

"Be careful, honey," I warned, and handed him the money. I watched in the mirror as he rushed over to the man and with a shy smile gave him the bill. I saw the man, startled, stand and take the money, putting it into his back pocket. *Good,* I thought to myself. *Now he will at least have a hot meal tonight.* I felt satisfied, proud of myself. I had made a sacrifice and now I could go on with my errands.

When Nick got back into the car, however, he looked at me

with sad, pleading eyes. "Mom, his dog looks so hot and the man is really nice." I knew I had to do more.

"Go back and tell him to stay there, that we will be back in fifteen minutes," I told Nick. He bounded out of the car and ran to tell the tattooed stranger.

We then drove to the nearest store and chose our gifts carefully. "It can't be too heavy," I explained to the children. "He has to be able to carry it around with him." We finally settled on our purchases: a bag of "Ol' Roy" (I hoped it was good—it looked good enough for me to eat! How do they make dog food look that way?), a flavored chew toy shaped like a bone, a water dish, bacon-flavored snacks (for the dog), two bottles of water (one for the dog, one for Mr. Tattoos), and some people snacks for the man.

We rushed back to the spot where we had left him, and there he was, still waiting. And still nobody else was stopping for him. With hands shaking, I grabbed our bags and climbed out of the car, all four of my children following me, each carrying gifts. As we walked up to him I had a fleeting moment of fear and hoped he wasn't a serial killer.

I looked into his eyes and saw something that startled me and made me ashamed of my judgment. I saw tears. He was fighting like a little boy to hold back his tears. How long had it been since someone had showed this man kindness? I told him I hoped it wasn't too heavy for him to carry and showed him what we had brought. He stood there like a child at Christmas, and I felt that my small contributions were so inadequate. When I took out the water dish, he snatched it out of my hands as if it were solid gold and told me he had had no way to give water to his dog. He gingerly set it down, filled it with the bottled water we brought, and stood up to look directly into my eyes. His were so blue, so intense. My own filled with tears as he said, "Ma'am, I don't know what to say." He then put both hands on his bandanna-clad head and just started to cry. This man—this "scary" man—was so gentle, so sweet, so humble.

I smiled through my tears and said, "Don't say anything." Then I noticed the tattoo on his neck. It said: "Mama tried."

As we all piled into the van and drove away, he was on his knees, arms around his dog, kissing the animal's nose and smiling. I waved cheerfully and then fully broke down into tears. I had so much. My worries seemed so trivial and petty now. I had a home, a loving husband, four beautiful children. I had a bed. I wondered where he would sleep that night.

My step-daughter, Brandie, turned to me and said in the sweetest little-girl voice, "I feel so good!"

Although it seemed that we had helped him, the man with the tattoos had really given us a gift that we would never forget. He had taught us that no matter what we look like on the outside, each of us is a child of God inside, deserving kindness, compassion, and acceptance. He opened my heart.

Tonight and every night I pray for the gentle man with the tattoos and his dog. And I hope that God will send more people like him into my life to remind me of what's really important.

Rebel with a "Claus"

GORDON SWENSEN

I used to stereotype Santa Claus as a big elf in red clothing who made toys, had a voracious appetite, and rubbed shoulders with little men. Santa Claus looked very different in a leather jacket, Levi jeans, and motorcycle boots. But there he was, a young James Dean, with all the trimmings of carefree rebellion. There was enough leather on him to refurbish an old couch. He was everything I had been told, as a sixteen-year-old, to avoid— the reason I should get an education, avoid drugs and alcohol, and prepare for a respectable career. Yet there was Jim, standing in our kitchen. But he seemed different up close. He had a genuine purpose for being there, and I was about to become the beneficiary of a lesson in acceptance.

Young Jim's life was anything but ordinary. He was raised by parents with strong moral, ethical, and religious values, but a rift must have occurred sometime during Jim's teenage years that changed his belief system and attitude. His manner of dress and his lifestyle were in sharp contrast to his upbringing. Jim even had had an occasional run-in with the law, developing an unfavorable reputation with some in the neighborhood.

I guess I had stereotyped him as well. To me, he seemed like a young time bomb filled with emotional gunpowder, poised to explode.

This particular Christmas, Jim's family was experiencing financial difficulties. With more than twenty individuals living in the home, including several children, the prospects of a joyous Christmas seemed unrealistic. But something glorious in Jim's heart found its way down the block, into our kitchen . . . an idea that gave him a reason to celebrate in his own way. Jim let our family in on a secret that was hard to contain. He worked for a local construction company and had saved his money in earnest.

He had decided to provide a memorable Christmas for his entire family. The prodigal son was going to kill the fatted calf for his own parents as a token of his love—a love that spread beyond pride, rebelliousness, and generational differences.

Parents, siblings, aunts, uncles, nephews, and nieces were not to be forgotten by Santa Claus this Christmas. Jim asked my mother if she would wrap the bundles of toys he had in his truck. The packages nearly filled the room. There were toasters and irons for the women, tools for the men, dolls and games for the children, and clothing for everyone. The packages went on and on. Jim even included an insignificant gift for himself, so that the identity of the unselfish giver would remain anonymous.

Then our "Santa in leather" turned to me and asked if I would serve as his elf and deliver the hallowed bounty to his home on Christmas Eve. A memorable night occurred shortly thereafter that afforded me, a young high school student, a glimpse at Christlike goodness. I parked the car, loaded with gifts, down the hill, out of view of their home. With my arms filled with packages, I carefully proceeded to decorate the front porch area with holiday joy. I felt a little like one of the Wise Men as I returned to the car for more of its precious cargo. Gold, frankincense, and myrrh rested in my arms on this cold winter's night adorned by Christmas lights, smoking chimneys, and houses filled with warmth and love.

I imagined Jim and his family downstairs singing Christmas carols around the tree, sharing holiday memories. The restless children would be dreaming about Christmas morning, the presents, and reindeer hooves on the rooftop. I also thought of the troubled parents, who knew that Santa would somehow forget to land on their house that night, the financial fog being too dense even for Rudolph's shiny nose.

When all the packages were in place, I knocked on the door and ran for cover under a large pine tree in the front yard. The door opened, and then it happened. I saw the faces of the children and heard their gleeful shouts. I saw the puzzled yet relieved looks of gratitude on the faces of the parents and their grown children.

And then I remember seeing Jim's countenance—the artificial look of surprise and the smile that seemed to have no end. It was then I forgot about the leather jacket, the boots, and the motorcycle. I forgot about the image, the attitude, and the discouraged delinquent. On that night, under peaceful skies, I heard angels sing, I saw hearts healed, I felt lives touched. I also learned that goodness comes in all sizes, colors, and shapes, and that below all the rough exteriors and artificial facades, there are, ofttimes, hearts pure as gold. Santa Claus came dressed in leather that Christmas long ago, riding a motorcycle, traveling his own road, and leaving a touch of Christmas magic on one young shepherd in search of a star.

"Where Was He?"

H. Burke Peterson

A few years ago I was assigned with other General Authorities to attend a series of area conferences in New Zealand and Australia. Initially, the leader of our group was to have been President Spencer W. Kimball. However, because of the need for some emergency surgery, he could not travel with us, so President N. Eldon Tanner led the group in his place.

Each day during the trip, President Tanner telephoned President Kimball in his hospital room to get a report on his condition and to give a short account of the conferences in which we were participating. After the daily call to Salt Lake City, President Tanner always described for us the President's condition. We were anxious and appreciated these brief messages.

Once, after we had been out for five or six days, President Tanner made his usual call to the hospital in Salt Lake City. However, this day he had nothing to relate to us about the prophet. When we asked if he had talked to him, he told us he had tried, but President Kimball wasn't in his room. "Where was he?" we asked. "They weren't sure; they couldn't find him," President Tanner said. "They thought he might have gone down to the next floor of the hospital to visit the sick."

A Moveable Feast

Elaine Cannon

The daffodils Nedra Warner had poked into a bean pot were for the centerpiece of a moveable feast that our son and his sons were to enjoy. His wife had just passed away, leaving three little boys below kindergarten age with their dad. Nedra had come to help the afflicted.

"Life can't be a picnic every day," she announced when the door opened and the four faced her, their frozen hearts matching the snowy day behind her. "But today you are going to have one!"

The mood changed when this rare and lovely neighbor swept in with a picnic basket crammed with all manner of delightful picnic fixings. And the daffodils. The children quickly caught the spirit and helped spread the checked cloth in the center of the living room floor. As a centerpiece, toddler Jared plunked himself down with the pot of daffodils, and the party was on.

What a departure—a picnic in the living room with Dad nodding approval! Nedra hadn't brought a casserole—not for a parlor picnic. She'd packed food fit for fussy children.

Cookie cutters had turned sandwiches into intriguing shapes—animals, angels, and stars. The names of the children were printed with cheese squeezed from a tube on the top of each sandwich. The carrot and celery strips were skinny slivers that a child could chew. Everything was prepared with the little ones in mind. Wisely, she let them discover the treats without the bustling about of the typical do-gooder. Nedra brought her moveable feast, her condolences, and left the bereaved family to enjoy their feast in privacy, all happier for her efforts.

Those Who Mix the Mortar

ARDETH G. KAPP

The plot of ground given to us to till is not always at the center of the stage.

Some years ago my husband, Heber, and I arose early to go to the laying of the cornerstone for the Jordan River Temple. We planned to arrive well before the crowd, but our plan was ill timed. The crowd was already there when we arrived. Due to the contour of the land, I was not only stretching to see over the heads of those in front of me, but we were on the low side of the slope in front of the temple, and I couldn't see what was going on. Heber, being considerably taller, tried to ease my disappointment by reporting to me observations from his vantage point. "The choir is assembling," he reported. "The General Authorities are taking their places. The TV cameras are in place." This only added to my frustration as I faced the backs of those in front who were seeing this historic event that I was missing.

After reaching and stretching without success, I decided to settle down, hoping to just feel the spirit of the occasion. It was when I relaxed that my perspective changed and I noticed an activity at the far northeast side of the temple. There I observed two men dressed in dark pants, white shirts, and ties, and each was holding a shovel. I saw them empty sacks of concrete into a wheelbarrow, pour in water, and mix the contents.

In time, after the choir sang and the presiding authorities had delivered impressive messages, Heber reported that the cameras were moving to the location for the placement of the cornerstone. At that moment the men who had been mixing the mortar pushed the wheelbarrow forward and quickly disappeared behind the scene. Then the cornerstone was anchored in place.

On the television news that evening, I saw what the cameras saw. But they did not see what I had seen. And even today, years later, I never drive past the Jordan River Temple without thinking of those men who mixed the mortar—those whose quiet, unsung labors played a major role in the placement of the cornerstone for the house of the Lord in a building that will stand against all of the storms of life.

Given a choice, would you be willing to serve with the men who mix the mortar? Small acts of service, small sacrifices, small notes and calls, words of encouragement one to another—these "small things" are the mortar that helps hold life together.

A Bottle of Warm Soda

Sandra Rogers

My deep interest in the field of international health and development and my choice of nursing as a career have taken me to many parts of the world. In the process I have learned many valuable lessons from men and women whose lives reflect Christ's teachings, even though they have no knowledge of the fulness of the gospel. One such lesson I learned in Nigeria.

Part of my work was an analysis of the strategies indigenous nurses used in meeting village health needs. On one occasion I went with a Nigerian nurse to do an initial family-health assessment. I did not speak Igbo and was an observer on this visit.

I can see clearly the reds of the dusty clay soil, the blues of the plastic water pitchers, the greens of the trees against a late afternoon sky. I can also feel the way the wind announced the coming of the rain that caused us to move our benches inside the small one-room home. I sat mostly in the corner with eyes like vacuums, pulling in every image: the two small cots along one wall, the faded curtain separating the parents' sleeping area from that of the five children, the small cupboard containing all the family belongings. I can see the wedding picture of the happy, young couple who hardly resembled the worried and fatigued parents talking with my Nigerian colleague. I can hear the rain on the corrugated tin roof. My nurse colleague explained that the mother had told her they had not eaten for two days because her husband was out of work and they were out of food.

As if on cue, the oldest child came in soaked to the skin (which didn't take much, given the thinness of his clothing), holding a rusty tray graced with two bottles of warm soda—gifts for the family's visitors. The parents insisted I take one. I was sitting on a stool so low my knees were in my ears, and directly across from me on the cots were the children, whose eyes were glued to the bottles of soda. I tried to graciously refuse this gift because I understood the terrible sacrifice the family was making in offering it to me. However, the father insisted, telling me that though he was poor and had no work, he still had his identity as an Igbo man and that I must not take that identity away by refusing his gift. Have any of you ever tried to drink something when all you could see over the lip of the bottle were the eyes of five hungry children? Next to giving up my sins, it is probably the hardest thing I will ever have to do. I drank very little and handed the bottle to the children because I was weeping so much I could not swallow. Every part of me ached with concern for this family and thousands like them, a concern that could only be communicated through my tears because I had no other language.

As we walked away from this visit, my heart was filled with prayers and my mind was filled with possible nursing interventions for this family. My Nigerian colleague said, "Do you want to know what that woman said? She told me that she never imagined that a white woman would come to visit her in her home. Moreover, she never believed that a white woman would cry with her. She said, 'If a white woman can cry with a black one, then maybe there is some hope for the world.'"

The Pure, the Bright, the Beautiful

Charles Dickens

The pure, the bright, the beautiful
    That stirred our hearts in youth,
The impulses to wordless prayer,
    The streams of love and truth,
The longing after something lost,
    The spirit's yearning cry,
The striving after better hopes—
    These things can never die.

The timid hand stretched forth to aid
    A brother in his need;
A kindly word in grief's dark hour
    That proves a friend indeed;
The plea for mercy softly breathed,
    When justice threatens high,
The sorrow of a contrite heart—
    These things shall never die.

Let nothing pass, for every hand
    Must find some work to do,
Lose not a chance to waken love—
    Be firm and just and true.
So shall a light that cannot fade
    Beam on thee from on high,
And angel voices say to thee—
    "These things shall never die."

"I Needed to Do a Good Deed"

ELAINE CANNON

Counting on God is a basic secret to emotional stability.

For example, there comes a time when your heart is broken, your spirit is sagging, your feeling of self-worth is thin. You admit that there is reason enough for such depression in this current set of circumstances. You deserve to be somewhat unstrung, even devastated. But you learned long ago that fruitless crying delays resolution to problems, and life is about problems. Therefore, it is good you've learned how to work through them, isn't it? So score one for you!

You check out your emotional symptoms to discover why you are weeping instead of being someone who stifles grief or hurt by dutifully doing one's duty no matter what milk is spilled. Whatever the details behind this particular trauma, the fact is that you are feeling blue because you are dwelling on the dark night with its disappointments. Instead, look to morning when joy cometh, thanks be to God who made the sun to rise as well as to set.

When you turn to the Lord in need and in increasing faith, the comfort always comes. It has never proven otherwise. That is the thing to remember. And when he has helped you, you quickly turn to help others.

A lovely lady named Linda came by to see me one frazzled, dumpy day. She had a pumpkin pie in hand.

"What have I done to deserve this?" I happily asked.

"I don't know, really. I needed to do a good deed, to live outside myself in love. Your name came to mind. Maybe I was inspired—who knows? Anyway, don't thank me, thank the Lord. But if the pie isn't good you can blame me!"

"What do you mean, you *needed* to do a good deed?"

"I woke up burdened with my grief. I'm just not used to being a widow yet, I guess, and I turned to the Lord, of course. You'd think he'd get so sick of me. Well, a few precious minutes of communion with God and I realized that though my husband wasn't resurrected at that moment, I wasn't alone. I had a few debts to pay, that's all, and so I needed to do a good deed."

And you know, that can be true with any of us. Maybe we need to do more good deeds to find ourselves "girded with gladness."

Carrying On

JANNA DeVore

At three in the morning, Beverly and Amber Williams, of McCammon, Idaho, are usually asleep. But July 1, 1996, wasn't a typical morning for these teenage sisters. Instead of sleeping, they were rushing their mom, Effie, to the hospital in nearby Soda Springs. About four hours later, their mom delivered a healthy baby boy. She named him David, after her husband and the girls' father, who was killed not long before in an industrial accident.

"We wanted to be there with my mom," says 16-year-old Beverly, "and to be with a brand-new baby who just came from where my dad is."

The girls stayed by their mom's side through the delivery and probably would have stayed at the hospital much longer if it weren't for one small problem: most of the baby clothes Effie had purchased were pink, for a girl. So Beverly and Amber hopped in the car and drove more than an hour to Pocatello to exchange the clothes. They also used their personal savings to buy a dresser for their new baby brother. They put the clothes and dresser in his room at home before returning to the hospital. Oh, and Beverly mowed the lawn first too. After all, Monday had always been the day that Effie mowed the lawn. Beverly knew her mom wouldn't be up to it.

Amber and Beverly seem to be around whenever their mom needs them these days. They help out willingly and do everything from balancing the checkbook to helping their younger sisters with homework.

On December 18, 1995, their dad was killed in an explosion at his work. He left behind five daughters and a wife, who later found out she was pregnant with their sixth child. Since then, the Williams family has survived on prayers and faith, along with help from the two oldest daughters.

"It was a really hard time, and I just knew that it wouldn't help anybody if I didn't do something to help out," says Beverly.

Amber, 14, agrees. "For the first couple of days we were so hurt and shocked that nobody could do anything, but then you realize it's real and you just can't sit around," she says.

"They basically took over for a while," Effie says. "They just didn't act like typical kids. They've had to do adult things. And instead of resenting the responsibility, they have done whatever's needed to be done."

Beverly says she likes the responsibility. She wanted to help her mom. She enjoys baby-sitting and running errands. She has even noticed the value of her math skills from doing things like balancing the checkbook. Amber also has a positive attitude about her responsibilities. She loves to spend time with her family, and baby-sitting the younger kids is her favorite way to help. She also says that diving into this type of service helped keep her mind on other things right after her dad's death.

Their dad, David Williams, was a man of strong character. He taught his children to work. He also taught them the gospel and showed them how to love one another.

Amber and Beverly see their contribution to the family as a way to follow that example. "I want to be like my dad in the way that he loved this life and loved people," Beverly says. "He's a good example for a lot of people. He cared about you and took time for you." Now, she and Amber are doing the same thing.

"We try to have fun times with our little sisters because their dad's gone now, and our dad helped us have fun when we were little," Amber says.

They also try to help out with the little things. At first that meant addressing thank-you notes after the funeral and doing the small but necessary things that their mom was too busy to do. Now that means doing some of the bigger things too, like getting ready for church on Sunday mornings.

With five girls, six including their mom, and only one bathroom, it's not hard to imagine what the Williams's house is like on Sunday mornings. "There's a lot to do," Amber says. "So we give the kids baths and help them get dresses on."

"They even help me with my Church calling if I'm busy with the baby," Effie says.

In everything they do, they remember their dad and his positive attitude and zest for life. It helps them to remember to work hard but to have fun too. "I know my dad will live on in my heart if I learn to love life as he did," says Beverly, "and I enjoy waking up to each new day with the bright intent that he had to make each day the greatest."

The girls are grateful for loving neighbors who invite their family to come on camping trips and go water skiing. They've learned how to snowboard. They hang out with friends. Mostly, they just realize that life can be very short; therefore, it's important to do what is right and be happy.

Faith was what pulled Amber and Beverly through those first few months and still helps them along today. "If I hadn't known the gospel was true then, I probably wouldn't have even wanted to live," Amber says. "But I have something to live for. I want to be a better person."

Beverly has similar feelings. "If I hadn't believed how I did then, I wouldn't have wanted to do anything. But I want to do my best so I can see my dad again."

Their new baby brother has given them a namesake for their dad. And, as babies usually do, he gave them reason to laugh and smile on a daily basis.

Their family has pulled through the initial shock and sorrow of David's death. That sadness will not go away soon, and it has permanently changed their lives, but the Williamses know that they can be happy and that their family can be together again.

They look at things in a positive way. "The kids have given me hope instead of giving up. They were so strong. David instilled that in them," Effie says.

Because David Williams did instill the basic principles and concepts of the gospel in his girls, they have made the best out of a difficult situation. They have followed his good example and blessed their family. They will continue to do so. They will do it for themselves and for their dad.

Editor's Note: The preceding selection was originally published in The New Era *magazine in October 1997. Since this story was written, Beverly, now eighteen, has graduated from high school and is training to become a dental assistant. She is also in the process of earning her private pilot's license. Amber is now sixteen and attending high school. Both girls are still very active in the Church and in their community. Their sisters Hope, Abby, and Dana enjoy watching their baby brother, David, grow. He's now three and a half. Effie, their mom, has since remarried.*

❧ THE *Workings* OF THE *Spirit*

She Heard the Blessing

H. Burke Peterson

Some years ago, when I was serving as a bishop in a ward in Arizona, we had an unusual group of teenagers. Most of them had the courage to do what was right. They stayed close to each other and helped each other when things got tough. Most of them went to a high school close by. In numbers, they were really only a handful of the total student body. They met a girl at the school who was not a member of the Church. Her circumstances were unusual, for she was deaf. She also had a defective heart. The only way she could know what you were saying was to watch your lips and read them. She sat in the front of each class so she could see the teacher speak. She was a good student, but when you can't hear and can't be active, it's hard for you to be a part of what is going on. You're sort of a spectator rather than a participant. She was a spectator watching from the sidelines.

The young people from the ward were friendly to her and invited her into their circle. She responded to their kindness. One step led to another, and with her parents' permission she was finally invited to receive the missionary lessons in one of the homes. She was taught by two nineteen-year-old Elders not much older than she. She liked what she heard; she believed what she heard; she felt good inside. The day was set for her baptism. We were all invited to go. Dressed in white, she and one of the missionaries entered the water, and she was baptized as he said, calling her by name, "Having been commissioned of Jesus Christ, I baptize you in the name of the Father, and of the Son, and of the Holy Ghost" (D&C 20:73).

The next step was for her to be confirmed. Some of us stood in the circle as priesthood hands were placed on her head. I was aware that she couldn't see the lips of the one confirming her. And she wouldn't be able to hear the blessing he might give. I listened carefully because I wanted to invite her into my office later, where she could see me talk and I could tell her what had been said.

A nineteen-year-old Elder was the voice as she was confirmed a member of the Church. He then continued with a blessing. As he spoke, he began to make her promises that I thought were unusual. In fact, I became a little uneasy at his words. He continued the blessing, and I began to feel a calm spirit of peace as he spoke. Later, I sat in front of her and said, "I want to tell you of the blessing the Elder gave you. It was tremendous."

She paused, and with moistened eyes said, "Bishop, I *heard* the blessing."

She had been healed. She could now hear, and her heart was beating normally. She could now participate more fully in the gospel and in the blessings of life.

There are many lessons to learn from this story. One is this: Here was a nineteen-year-old missionary, an Elder holding the holy Melchizedek Priesthood. He had *prepared* himself for a mission. He had *made himself worthy* to be an instrument in the hands of the Lord to perform a miracle. So, as he stood with his hands on her head, he felt an impression—a heavenly message, if you please—telling him there was a special blessing for this young woman and he had been chosen to deliver it.

He listened. He obeyed. And through the authority and power of the priesthood, a young life was made whole.

The Recommend

GEORGE D. DURRANT

In the days that followed my mission call, the excitement carried me along. I was treated in the special way that people treat those who are soon to leave on missions. Then there was a long series of thrills—buying a navy blue suit, being photographed for a missionary picture, having a farewell where girls came that I didn't even know cared, shaking hands until my own hand ached from grasping the hands of hundreds (though it seemed like thousands) of well-wishers.

Then the mission home. (When I went on my mission, we went to the mission home in Salt Lake.) I'll always remember the mission home.

"Tomorrow morning we go to the temple," the mission president said. "You all were told to bring your recommends and so we know you did."

Then it hit me. In all my preparation I'd forgotten to get a recommend. I felt sick. I panicked: I'll probably be sent home before I even leave Utah. How could I be so dumb? I don't dare tell the president.

Shortly thereafter the meeting ended. Others headed for the evening meal. I ran toward downtown Salt Lake City. I've never been more upset. I saw a phone booth. I entered. I'd call my bishop. He'd help. He lived in American Fork, some thirty-five miles away, but he worked for the highway patrol. I'd call the highway patrol. In the Yellow Pages I searched for the number. "Oh, no!" There were at least fifteen different numbers. My finger trembled as it moved from one number to the next. I prayed, "Oh, please, let me call the right place." I decided on a number and dialed it. "Highway patrol," a woman's voice answered.

"I . . . ah was . . . well . . . I'm trying to reach Mel Grant."

"Mel Grant," she said in a surprised voice. "How did you know he was here?" I said I didn't know. She said, "He almost never comes here, but he's here now."

A moment later I was speaking to my bishop. (Bishops are good to have.) I told him of my plight. He said, "I'll go right home, get the recommend, get it to the stake president, and then give it to a patrolman who'll rush it to you."

That night in the evening session a patrolman entered the back of the hall. All eyes were fixed upon him as he made his way to the stand and whispered to the mission president. The president then arose, interrupted the speaker, and stated, "This man desires to see Elder Durrant."

I arose, and as I began to walk to the foyer I felt the stare of each one in the room. A moment later the patrolman gave me my glorious ticket. A ticket to the temple, which for me was the beginning of a testimony. That night my prayers were quite intense. It felt good to know that the Lord took care of one young man who needed help so desperately.

Too Busy to Listen

HAROLD B. LEE

President [David O.] McKay related to the Twelve an interesting experience. . . .

He said it is a great thing to be responsive to the whisperings of the Spirit, and we know that when these whisperings come it is a gift and our privilege to have them. They come when we are relaxed and not under pressure of appointments. (I want you to mark that.) The President then took occasion to relate an experience in the life of Bishop John Wells, former member of the Presiding Bishopric.

A son of Bishop Wells was killed in Emigration Canyon on a railroad track. . . . Sister Wells was inconsolable. She mourned during the three days prior to the funeral, received no comfort at the funeral, and was in a rather serious state of mind.

One day soon after the funeral services while she was lying on her bed relaxed, still mourning, she said her son appeared to her and said, "Mother, do not mourn, do not cry. I am all right." He told her that she did not understand how the accident happened and explained that he had given the signal to the engineer to move on, and then made the usual effort to catch the railing on the freight train; but as he attempted to do so his foot caught on a root and he failed to catch the handrail, and his body fell under the train. It was clearly an accident.

Now, listen. He said that as soon as he realized that he was in another environment he tried to see his father, *but couldn't reach him. His father was so busy with the duties in his office he could not respond to his call.* Therefore he had come to his mother. He said to her, "You tell Father that all is well with me, and I want you not to mourn anymore."

Then the President made the statement that the point he had in mind was that when we are relaxed in a private room we are more susceptible to those things; and that so far as he was concerned, his best thoughts come after he gets up in the morning and is relaxed and thinking about the duties of the day; that impressions come more clearly, as if it were to hear a voice. Those impressions are right. If we are worried about something and upset in our feelings, the inspiration does not come. If we so live that our minds are free from worry and our conscience is clear and our feelings are right toward one another, the operation of the Spirit of the Lord upon our spirit is as real as when we pick up the telephone.

$\mathscr{L}$istening to the Conscience

STEPHEN R. COVEY

In an Arizona university at a "Religion of Life" week, I was invited to be a representative of our church, along with representatives of other churches. The second evening there I was asked to speak to a sorority/fraternity exchange at the Chi Omega House on the subject of the New Morality. Basically I gave the Church's approach to it: that chastity is an eternal law, that the new morality is really the old immorality, and so forth. But the feelings and views of the audience seemed to be against this, and I felt very alone. Two young men in particular were extremely articulate in expressing their opposition to my position. One on the front row said, basically, "Well, it seems to me that true, mature love gives more freedom than you're allowing."

I tried to reason with them, suggesting that chastity is an eternal principle—a law, a natural law, just as gravity is. I indicated that if you were to take poison unaware, its effects would nevertheless proceed, and that likewise unchastity would bring many negative consequences, personal and social, regardless of awareness. The front row young man argued against this, again from the viewpoint that this didn't give the kind of freedom a careful, mature, responsible love would give. Several others spoke against my position. One said I had no right to judge right or wrong for others.

Finally I asked the audience, "Would you listen for just a minute, and if you don't inwardly sense this principle to be true, I'll leave and not waste more of your time. I'll ask a question, then let's be still and listen—and I assure you that you'll inwardly sense that what I've been saying about chastity is true."

They became quite still. Some of them were looking around to see who was going to take my request seriously. I pressed the point: "Just listen for one minute."

At the beginning of that quiet minute, I asked the question: "Is chastity, as I have explained it, a true principle or not?" I paused. At the end of a full minute I turned to the fellow in the front and asked, "My friend, in all honesty, what did you feel? What did you hear?"

He replied, "What I heard is not what I've been saying."

I asked another, "What did you hear?"

"I don't know," he said. "I just don't know anymore."

Independently and spontaneously, a young man at the back stood and said, "I want to say something to my fraternity brothers I've never said before. I believe in God." And he sat down.

A completely different spirit was now present. It softened everybody. From then on it was easy to teach and testify. Many were very interested in the restored gospel and the Book of Mormon. We invited many to the institute of religion and gave several books out.

In that one moment, those who had really listened had heard (felt) the still, small voice, which cultural and social conditioning or programming had tried to silence through sophisticated and impressive orchestration. From then on it was up to them which voice they would listen to, which education they would accept.

She Prayed for Whatever She Would Like

SHIRLEY W. THOMAS

A special experience was shared with me by a dear sister many years ago after a sacrament meeting in the Hyde Park chapel in London—an experience with prayer. Deciding what to ask in our prayers is one of the important choices we have. Reading of the Nephite disciples of Jesus being given the words to pray suggests to us how the Holy Ghost has guided others (see 3 Nephi 19:24). That is sometimes called praying in the Spirit (see D&C 46:28, 30).

That Sunday in London was in June 1978, the weekend of the announcement of the revelation on the priesthood. I happened to be in England on a Relief Society assignment. The lovely sister I spoke with was the mother of two boys of Aaronic Priesthood age. The family was of African heritage. At the sacrament meeting, just finished, these two newly ordained priesthood holders had passed the sacrament for the first time. The tearful mother was receiving expressions of love from the also-tearful ward members. They shared her joy. Those two young men had faithfully attended priesthood meetings, hoping for the day they could fully participate. I knew how faithfully because one of our sons, participating in the BYU semester abroad in London the year before, had taught the teachers quorum in the ward. He had written from London to tell us about his class that each week consisted of three boys, two of whom were the sons of this woman. He had told us particularly of his admiration for the dedication and devotion of those two young men.

As the people in the foyer dispersed, the mother of the boys told the small group remaining that only a few days before, as she was praying, she had received the extraordinary invitation by the Spirit that she might ask whatever she would like. With her eyes brimming, she told us how overwhelmed she had been by the experience. She had always tried to feel the direction of the Spirit in her prayers and had never felt it appropriate to ask for the priesthood for her sons, even though that had always been what she really wanted. Now, after this experience was followed so soon by the announcement from Church headquarters, she realized that while the revelation was for the entire Church, the Lord acknowledged her individual hopes and addressed them personally. The Holy Ghost had invited her to pray for whatever she would like, knowing that this most important desire could now be realized.

Spirit Letters

SHELDON L. ANDERSON

Though others have her company,
She cares for us, just as before.
She knows our hurt and loneliness,
But would not have us grieving more.

Remember how with faithfulness
She wrote her love with shaky pen?
So even now, from time to time,
She sends her love to us again.

We would not cry for written word,
And now she'd have us understand
Our memories and thoughts of her
Are "spirit letters" from her hand.

The Wrestle

HUGH B. BROWN

I was asked to come down from Canada to Salt Lake City at a time when I was drilling oil wells, at a time when I thought I was almost a millionaire, a time when it looked as if nothing could save me from becoming a millionaire. I didn't want to be saved from the downdrag of money, but I had at that time a sort of feeling that I wanted to know whether it was right for me to pursue the course I was taking. I awoke one morning about three o'clock—mornings come early up there in the summertime. I was in a little cottage up in the Canadian Rockies. I was worried, bothered. I got out of my bed, dressed, and went up into the mountains, far back in the hills, remembering that the Savior often went to the mountains for his communications with his Father.

When I got up in the mountains on top of a peak, I was all alone, and I removed my hat and said, "Oh, God, are you there? You know that I am about to be a millionaire, or I think I am. Father, if this would not be good for me or my family, don't allow it to happen. If it is going to rob my family of their faith, don't allow it to happen." I talked to him as a man would talk to another man. I didn't seem to get an answer. I stayed up there for some time.

I drove back to Edmonton that evening; and upon arriving I said to Sister Brown, "I think I'll not want any supper tonight. I think I'll go in the back bedroom and sleep. You had better stay in the other room because I fear I am going to have a troubled night."

I went into that bedroom and closed the door, and I became conscious of a blackness such as I had never known. There was something in that room that made me feel very sincerely that I would like to be rubbed out—I would like to cease to be. I didn't think of suicide, but I did think seriously that if there were any way that I could be washed out, that would be the best thing that could happen to me.

I spent the night in that attitude, in that aura of awful blackness. Early in the morning Sister Brown came in—she had heard me walking the floor. When she closed the door she said, "My goodness, my dear! What's in this room?"

I said, "The devil is in this room, and he is trying to destroy me."

Together we knelt at the bedside and prayed for guidance and deliverance. We didn't seem to get it. Next morning I went down to my office in the city. It was Saturday. I knew no one would be there, and I wanted to be alone. I knelt by my cot and pleaded with God for deliverance, for that awful blackness was still on my soul. And it seemed to me that the sun came up. I obtained peace of soul, serenity of spirit. I phoned Sister Brown and told her, "Everything is all right. I don't know what happened, but it's all right."

That night I was taking a bath (You remember I told you that it was Saturday?) when the telephone rang. Sister Brown came to the door and said, "Salt Lake is calling."

I said, "Who in the dickens wants to talk to me at this time of night?" It was 10:30. I went to the phone. When I said, "Hello," I heard a voice which said, "This is David O. McKay calling."

I said, "Yes, President McKay."

"The Lord wants you to give the balance of your life to the Church. Tomorrow will be the closing session of Conference. Can you get here in time for the afternoon session?"

I told him I couldn't, as there were no planes flying.

He said, "Come as soon as you can."

I hung up, and that night—this was the night following the night of agony—Sister Brown and I spent another wakeful night, but it was a night of ecstasy. Not that we were looking for position, but to think that the God of heaven would reach out 1,200 miles and touch a man on the shoulder and say, "Come!" and to think that I would be that man, was almost more than I could understand!

When I came down to Salt Lake thirty days later I told the President about my awful experience and he said, "As far as I know, every man that is called into the General Authorities has to wrestle with the devil." You have to have a lot of courage if you come out victorious.

Ralph

ROBERT E. WELLS

Ralph came into the family history center in Arizona for help. He was a product of the "orphan trains" around the turn of the century. His brother Frank was seven, his sister Edna was five, and Ralph was three years old when they were placed in the New York Foundling Home. Three months later they were sent to Minnesota on a train. They were placed on a movie theater stage in a small town so that local people could pick out the children they wanted to take into their homes. Each child was sent to a different home.

By the time Ralph was ten years old, his brother and sister had moved away and he never saw them again. All his life he wondered why they had been left at the orphanage. He also wanted to know his real name. He pleaded with Sister Shelley at the family history center to help him in his task.

Sister Shelley felt prompted to use all the Church's resources to aid Ralph. She studied the 1900 New York Census Soundex for hours. Despite the hundreds of rolls of film in this census, she found nothing that might be a lead. This dedicated worker decided the assignment was impossible without more information available only from the other side of the veil. She retired to a quiet place to pray and asked the Lord to guide her in finding Ralph's family. She felt the impression to leave the film she was working on, change to a new film, and look under the name "Truck."

Forty-five minutes later she came across the family of Frank and Edna "Turck," ages twenty-seven and twenty-five, with three children named Frank, Edna, and Ralph. Although the spelling was not exactly the same, it was close enough for Sister Shelley to spot it. The names of the children were identical, so she felt this had to be the right family. Further investigation confirmed that it was indeed the name she needed. No one can explain why the Spirit told her to look for "Truck" when in fact she should have been seeking "Turck," but it was close enough. There was no doubt that the heavens had opened, and a major miracle had occurred.

Sister Shelley, now knowing the real last name of the family, called the New York Foundling Home. They pulled their files and told her that identical letters to each child had been placed in their files in the event they ever contacted the agency.

In this letter to Ralph, the father stated that his wife had died in 1901, and that he was very ill and did not expect to live long. He said he was writing to explain what had happened and how much he loved each child.

Sister Shelley, writing the above story, adds, "Each time I relate this story of Ralph Richardson Turck, I am reminded of how much our Heavenly Father and our Savior Jesus Christ love us. We were able to give Ralph three generations of names on each side from the records at the Foundling Home. And Ralph was really one year younger than he thought he was."

The Radio Analogy

Harold B. Lee

Some years ago . . . I served as a stake president. We had a very grievous case that had to come before the high council and the stake presidency that resulted in the excommunication of a man who had harmed a lovely young girl. After a nearly all-night session that resulted in that action, I went to my office rather weary the next morning and was confronted by a brother of this man whom we had had on trial the night before. This man said, "I want to tell you that my brother wasn't guilty of what you charged him with."

"How do you know he wasn't guilty?" I asked.

"Because I prayed, and the Lord told me he was innocent," the man answered.

I asked him to come into the office and we sat down, and I asked, "Would you mind if I ask you a few personal questions?"

He said, "Certainly not."

"How old are you?"

"Forty-seven."

"What priesthood do you hold?"

He said he thought he was a teacher.

"Do you keep the Word of Wisdom?"

"Well, no." He used tobacco, which was obvious.

"Do you pay your tithing?"

He said, "No"—and he didn't intend to as long as that blankety-blank-blank man was the bishop of the Thirty-Second Ward.

I said, "Do you attend your priesthood meetings?"

He replied, "No, sir!" and he didn't intend to as long as that man was bishop.

"You don't attend your sacrament meetings either?"

"No, sir."

"Do you have your family prayers?" and he said no.

"Do you study the scriptures?" He said well, his eyes were bad, and he couldn't read very much.

I then said to him: "In my home I have a beautiful instrument called a radio. When everything is in good working order we can dial it to a certain station and pick up the voice of a speaker or a singer all the way across the continent or sometimes on the other side of the world, bringing them into the front room as though they were almost right there. But after we have used it for a long time, the little delicate instruments or electrical devices on the inside called radio tubes begin to wear out. When one of them wears out, we may get some static—it isn't so clear. Another wears out, and if we don't give it attention, the sound may fade in and out. And if another one wears out—well, the radio may sit there looking quite like it did before, but because of what has happened on the inside, we can hear nothing.

"Now," I said, "you and I have within our souls something like what might be said to be a counterpart of those radio tubes. We might have what we call a 'go-to-sacrament-meeting' tube, a 'keep-the-Word-of-Wisdom' tube, a 'pay-your-tithing' tube, a 'have-your-family-prayers' tube, a 'read-the-scriptures' tube, and, as one of the most important—one that might be said to be the master tube of our whole soul—we have what we might call the 'keep-yourselves-morally-clean' tube. If one of these becomes worn out by disuse or inactivity—if we fail to keep the commandments of God—it has the same effect upon our spiritual selves that a worn-out tube has in a radio.

"Now, then," I said, "fifteen of the best-living men in the Pioneer Stake prayed last night. They heard the evidence and every man was united in saying that your brother was guilty. Now you, who do none of these things, you say you prayed and got an opposite answer. How would you explain that?"

Then this man gave an answer that I think was a classic. He said, "Well, President Lee, I think I must have gotten my answer from the wrong source." And, you know, that's just as great a truth as we can have. We get our answers from the source of the power we list to obey. If we're following the ways of the devil, we'll get answers from the devil. If we're keeping the commandments of God, we'll get our answers from God.

Faith AND Prayer

$\mathscr{T}$he Contact Lens

Richard H. Cracroft

There are a multitude of patterns which frame the finger of the Lord in our lives and bring His ways and means into focus. One of the patterns that has guided me in exercising personal faith first smacked me in the right eye as a young missionary. President Harold B. Lee named it best when he taught us to "walk to the edge of the light, and perhaps a few steps into the darkness, and you will find that the light will appear and move ahead of you." That step into the dark is the start-up key to an act of faith. Thus the brother of Jared prepared sixteen stones and, from the darkness of mortality but with the brightness of faith, asked, "Touch these stones, O Lord, with thy finger, and prepare them that they may shine forth in darkness" (Ether 3:4). And the Lord flooded Mahonri Moriancumer (the real name of the brother of Jared) and his people with light. It is a pattern: faith precedes the miracle, as darkness precedes dawn—just as it did when Peter forgot himself and stepped out of that ship and into the darkness to walk upon the sea (see Matthew 14:29); just as it did recently when I, as home teacher, taught the "One Step into the Dark Pattern" to a large and faithful family by blindfolding the four-year-old daughter, standing her on a table, and asking her to fall off the table into the waiting arms of her daddy. Without a moment's hesitation, and despite the obvious squeamishness of her older brothers and sisters, the little girl stood tall and fell headlong into the darkness—where she was safely caught by her father. She had taken that step into the dark—and was duly rewarded by a glad (and relieved) home teacher.

So it was for me, when, on a rainy summer afternoon in 1958, I unwittingly traced the "One Step into the Dark Pattern" while tracting along a gravel road on a hillside above Baden, Switzerland. As we walked from home to home, I was suddenly laid low by a speck of dust in my right eye. I learned, as one who had worn brand-new contact lenses for only five days, that a mote feels like a beam. I quickly extracted the lens, cleaned and rewetted it, and prepared to reinsert it. But as I held my finger at the ready, a gust of wind suddenly swept the lens from my fingertip: My lens was gone with the wind. I stood aghast—and virtually blind, being plunged instantly into 20/600 vision in one eye, which had been miraculously corrected to 20/20 only a week earlier.

Elder Neil Reading and I began to search on hands and knees in the wet gravel, sweeping an eight-foot radius from my supposed point of loss. We searched futilely for twenty minutes. Then, half-blind and half-despairing, I suggested to my companion that while we were already in position, we should pray. I reasoned with the Lord, told him about my need to see; about our need to meet our three investigator families that evening; about my feeling that there was more to be gained by finding the lens than by my learning whatever I was to learn from the loss. As I concluded the prayer and stood up, I received one of those Joseph Smith "flashes of intelligence." It surprised me, but I reacted at once. Explaining the revealed plan to my startled companion, I stood on my feet in the same place I had stood earlier, squeezed out my left contact lens, and was instantly plunged into the distorted, virtual blindness of 20/600 vision. I had begun my step into the dark.

Assured that my companion was on his knees and at the ready, I put my left lens in my mouth, extracted it, and, mounting it on my finger some six inches from my face, I waited—but not for long. A slight breeze caught my left lens, and it was gone. My step into the dark was now complete. I stood stock-still, heart in throat, until Elder Reading said, "I see it. It's still in the air."

"Don't lose it," I pled, and held my breath.

"It's still up," he whispered, now ten feet away. Then, from even further away, he exclaimed, "It's starting to fall!"

"Keep your eye on it," I pled again, wringing my hands in apprehension.

"I see it! I see it!" he said. There was a long pause—of three hours or seconds—and then, "Oh my gosh! Oh my gosh!"

I braced.

"Oh my gosh," he repeated; "it's landed, and"—pause . . . pause . . . pause—". . . almost right on top of the other lens!"

"You see the other lens?" I shouted.

"Yes, it's right here!"

The darkness was flooded with light.

Unable to see a thing, I crawled over to him on hands and knees. Slowly, he planted in my palm, in order, my left and right lenses—my seer stones. I wet the lenses and, with my back to the wind and sheltered by my companion's hovering frame, I implanted them: "And there was light, and it was good." And we knelt, full of gratitude, and I thanked our God for tender and tangible mercies. We pressed on to the next house, filled with wonder at a God who knows each sparrow's fall *and* the exact whereabouts in Baden, Switzerland, of Elder Cracroft's right contact lens.

Determined to Be Worthy

H. Burke Peterson

At a stake conference, the stake president called a young father, who had just been ordained an elder, from the audience to bear his testimony. The father had been active in the Church as a boy, but during his teenage years had veered somewhat from his childhood pattern. After returning from the military service, he married a lovely girl, and presently children blessed their home.

Without warning an undisclosed illness overcame their little four-year-old daughter. Within a very short time she was on the critical list in the hospital. In desperation and for the first time in many years the father went to his knees in prayer, asking that her life be spared. As her condition worsened and he sensed that she would not live, the tone of the father's prayers changed. He no longer asked that her life be spared, but rather for a blessing of understanding: "Let thy will be done," he said.

Soon the child was in a coma, indicating her hours on earth were few. Now, fortified with understanding and trust, the young parents asked for one more favor of the Lord. Would he allow her to awaken once more that they might hold her closely? The little one's eyes opened, her frail arms outstretched to her mother and then to her daddy for a final embrace. When the father laid her on the pillow to sleep till another morning, he knew their prayers had been answered—a kind, understanding Father in Heaven had filled their needs as he knew them to be. His will had been done; they had gained understanding. They were determined now to live worthily that they might live again with her.

Do you remember the words of the Lord to the Prophet Joseph Smith when he was having that great test of his faith in the Liberty Jail? The Lord said, "If thou art called to pass through tribulation . . ." and then called to the Prophet's mind a series of possibilities that would test any man to the utmost. Then the Lord concluded, "Know thou, my son, that all these things shall give thee experience, and shall be for thy good" (D&C 122:5, 7).

It's interesting to note that from the depths of trial and despair have come some of the most beautiful and classic passages of modern-day scripture—not from the ease of a comfortable circumstance. Might this also be the case in our own lives! From trial comes refined beauty.

Strong Son of God

From *In Memoriam*

ALFRED, LORD TENNYSON

Strong Son of God, immortal Love,
    Whom we, that have not seen thy face,
    By faith, and faith alone, embrace,
Believing where we cannot prove;

We have but faith: we cannot know,
    For knowledge is of things we see;
    And yet we trust it comes from thee,
A beam in darkness: let it grow.

To Cope with Things I Would Not Choose

ARDETH G. KAPP

The sacred mission of teaching and the ultimate joys that attend—those most lasting, those felt most deeply—are often borne out of struggle, anxiety, and determination that is sustained only through unwavering faith in God. The moments of greatest anxiety can become forerunners to the deepest joy and ultimate ecstasy when a mother teaches her own child. In the inspiring example of Ruth Yancey, as she has dedicated her life to teaching her children, and especially her son Steven, I witnessed evidence of this great joy borne out of struggle.

In the first few days after Steven's birth, Sister Yancey and her husband began suspecting something might be wrong with their precious baby, although he had gained several pounds since his two-pound, eleven-ounce birth weight. An ophthalmologist confirmed the young couple's grave concern. Heavy doses of oxygen used to save his life were more than the tiny blood vessels of his eyes could stand. Those blood vessels had ruptured, and he was blind.

One morning after her husband had gone to work, Sister Yancey cradled her son close to her and began pleading with the Lord. "Help me to know how to teach him, what to say, how to show him so he can accomplish each task," she prayed. "Inspire me, because I am your tool in teaching this special spirit. I'm weak. I'm uneducated. I'm unknowledgeable about what should be done. Help me to know what to do and how Steven and I can accomplish it."

With faith in God, this dedicated mother willingly and anxiously shouldered the responsibility of teacher and walked carefully into those first fundamental lessons. "We thought that when children got teeth they'd know how to chew," she said, "but they don't. Children learn from imitation, by seeing others chew. So I would put food in my mouth and place his little hands on my jaws and chew. Then I would put food in his mouth. He would spit it out or start to choke, but after a while he began to learn how to manipulate his jaws." Months later she realized the joy of that first accomplishment—he had learned how to chew.

When her son was just a little older, this faithful young mother had to prepare for other lessons, one after the other. "In teaching Steven to walk, I couldn't say, 'Walk to your daddy,' because he couldn't see his daddy. So we bought a little push toy for him that we called his lawn mower. He learned to walk with that. He wouldn't dare walk around the house without it, because he was afraid he would bump into something."

While the lessons were very difficult for the child, it was his mother who had to be willing to suffer if the next hurdle were to be crossed.

"When Steven was two years old," she continued, "we built a fence around our backyard so he would have a protected area to play in, and I would feel more secure about his safety. The plan was good only for a while, until the day when he found his way to the gate. Day after day he would stand at the gate and cry."

Sister Yancey told how she and her devoted husband together found the strength to do what had to be done. They bought Steven a little toy truck with a steering wheel and a seat. When he sat on the truck his feet touched the ground, and he could "walk-ride" the truck down the sidewalk. This provided something he could hold onto and something that would be ahead of him and protect him from falling in case of interference in his path.

"The first few times I would open the gate and let him out on the sidewalk alone, then go into the house and watch the clock. I would tell myself that I must not check on him for two full minutes. I would force myself to let him be gone for two long minutes at a time, then I would run out to see if he was still on the sidewalk and going in the right direction. Then I would go back into the house and wait another two full minutes."

Gradually, with faith, the teacher's confidence in herself and her child grew. Steven would go to the end of the block and turn around and come back. In time it was two full blocks. Without the struggle required to open the gate, the rewards and victory might have been withheld, to the detriment of mother and child.

In the events of those very early years, there were also moments of great joy. About two months after Steven's second birthday, the Yanceys moved into a new home. Steven and his four-year-old brother, John, were playing in the living room while their parents were busy putting things away. Suddenly Brother and Sister Yancey heard "America" being played on the piano. Both came running into the living room. "We thought John must be playing the piano. But it was not John. We just stood there. It was like a miracle. This baby for whom we had concerns about brain damage, his hearing, his sight, and all those kinds of things, was playing 'America' in octaves with his third fingers resting on the tops of his index fingers on both hands just to get enough strength to play the notes."

From then on young Steven could duplicate on the piano the melody of any music he heard. He played hymns, nursery rhymes, popular music. By the time he was four or five he could play almost anything, but still just in octaves. "Whenever I played the piano he would climb up on my lap and lightly place his little hands on each of my arms so it didn't restrict me at all, but he could feel the movement of my playing. It was so easy to teach him music, whereas most of the things I taught him were quite a struggle. We worked; we had frustrations; we both had tears. Sometimes we wondered if we were going to make it—like the effort to help him learn to tie his shoes—but teaching him music was a joy."

When Steven was a little older, his parents, anxious to provide maximum opportunities for him, purchased a second piano. Sister Yancey, an accomplished musician, would sit at one piano and he would sit at the other. "No matter what I would play, how big the chord, or how long the phrases, he would always be just a split second behind me. He would learn it and memorize it as we would go. His mind is like a tape recorder; once a piece is there, it is not forgotten."

During Steven's senior year in high school, he took a class in music history and composition in which he had to orchestrate a song. He chose "Sunrise, Sunset" from *Fiddler on the Roof*. He wrote the parts for all the instruments in a full band—twenty different scores. Together Steven and his mother discussed the characteristics and voice range of each instrument. He would experiment on the piano until he could decide what he wanted each instrument to do. Then he would dictate that part to his mother, and she would transcribe it on staff paper. Together they would transpose it to the key of that instrument. "With his ear, having perfect pitch, and my eyes, we made a pretty good team. I couldn't have done that without him and he couldn't have done it without me. What a thrill it was when the Viewmont High School concert band played it for us. There have been many such times of great joy.

"Graduation from high school presented more challenges. The ceremony was to be held in a very large auditorium. The custodian told us which ramp the graduates would be using, and where they would leave the stage. So Steven and his father and I counted the steps from the end of the carpeted ramp over to the table where he would receive his diploma, and from there over to the other ramp. We walked through it together many times. His dad would guide him up the ramp, Steven would walk the full width of the stage unhesitatingly by himself, and I would be there at the other ramp to receive him. This way Steven would be getting that diploma all by himself."

The graduating class that year was large, and the conducting officer requested that there be no applause. Well, there was no applause until they announced Steven's name—then the whole senior class stood up and applauded. Steven not only received his diploma, he also received a college scholarship in music. "It was one of the proudest and happiest moments of my life," his mother said. "It really was."

For a young bird, pushed gently from the security of the nest, there comes a time for the solo flight, when the teacher must stand in the wings trusting that the teaching has been sufficient for the immediate challenge, and wings are spread in flight and there is no turning back. It was at the airport that Steven made final preparations for his solo flight. His mother and father, brothers and sister would remain behind. He had accepted a call to serve the Lord on a two-year mission to the Anaheim California Mission. Steven grabbed the handrail and made his way carefully into the big jetliner that would take him away to unfamiliar places. "As he left my side I got such a feeling of peace," his mother recalled. "It was that feeling of putting him into the hands of the Lord, as the Lord had put him into my hands. I had done my best, and now I knew the Lord would care for him."

Instead of waiting for two full minutes after opening the gate, this trusting mother was prepared, with peace in her heart, to wait two full years with less anxiety than the two full minutes had previously demanded. Much, much learning had taken place. "I feel pride in him, and sometimes pride in myself that I was able to help him. But that is secondary. The most important thing is the feeling of gratitude, even to the point where I'm grateful for those hard things to learn and to teach. Life could be easier and more pleasant if we didn't have struggles, but we don't grow much that way." This great teacher expressed her joy and gratitude by saying, "I'm thankful I've had the chance to cope with things I would not have chosen to cope with because we've all learned so much."

A Generous Employer

KEVIN STOKER

As they walked along a New England country road in the mid-1940s, Elders Truman Madsen and Reuel J. Bawden wondered where they would get their next meal.

The missionaries "were rather unpopular among these farm folk," writes Elder Madsen of the experience. The two missionaries had spent the night sleeping in a barn and hadn't eaten in twenty-four hours. So they left the road and entered a grove of trees to pray for help in getting something to eat.

"This happened often in our country work—going off into the woods to pray," writes Elder Madsen. "It wasn't a habit—it was a necessity. Who but the Lord could help us in these hostile country areas? We were without purse or scrip. But He in whose work we were engaged was ever within reach, the unfailing source."

In prayer, Elder Bawden pleaded, "Father, wilt thou open the way for us to have a bite to eat."

As they arose, the Elders saw a trout jump and strike a fly in the small brook flowing through the grove of trees.

"O for a fishing pole!" Elder Madsen muttered.

"What's wong with what you have in your hands?" queried Elder Bawden.

The tattered umbrella didn't look like much, but it was all they had. Elder Bawden doubled up some thread and attached a doctored safety pin to the end while his companion located a worm. Elder Madsen then gave the contraption a try.

Dangling the line over the grassy bank, he thought, "Can this be the way the Lord is going to answer our prayer . . . , or do I just have a flair for the unusual?"

He already knew the answer. The Lord had answered their prayers before, so there was no reason why he couldn't arrange for a fish to bite.

Wham! A trout struck hard. Elder Madsen jerked, and a fish flew over his head, off the hook and onto the bank. As they looked for more worms, tears filled their eyes.

They caught and cooked six fish, offering heartfelt thanks to the Lord before eating them, fins and all.

"You know," said Elder Bawden as he picked up his suitcase, "the Lord is a mighty generous employer."

The Snowstorm

RANDAL A. WRIGHT

Wendy came to me in October of 1995 to apply for a temple sealing cancellation. She was a humble and faithful member of the Church. She was now engaged to be married to a fine man but needed clearance from the First Presidency to be sealed. She was counseled not to set a specific date for the marriage because it was uncertain when the clearance would be considered. However, she planned to move out of the country with her new husband, and the marriage date had to be set. We included a date in the request, understanding that if the clearance was not received in time, the couple would be married in the temple for time only. The marriage was scheduled for January. We were sure clearance would be granted by that time.

The final papers were sent by the stake president in November. By the end of November no word had been received. By the end of December I had serious doubts about whether or not the clearance would come. On January 13, we called Salt Lake City to find out if the department that handles these cases had any word from the First Presidency. They said that things were going a little slow, for those involved were participating in the dedication of the Bountiful Temple. Knowing that Monday was a holiday and that they would not be meeting until Tuesday at 8:00 A.M. (the exact date and time of the marriage), I felt there was no chance for the sealing to take place and told this sister that she should plan for a sealing at a later time.

Having faith, she fasted and prayed that a miracle would happen. Tuesday morning arrived and the couple went to the Salt Lake Temple to be married for time only. Temple workers placed tags on the couple when they arrived that said "Married for Time." When the appointed hour arrived for the marriage, however, there was a problem. A huge snowstorm in the Salt Lake area had delayed several of the wedding guests. Wendy and her husband-to-be were upset, knowing that these people would not be present for the wedding. The temple workers discussed the situation and decided to delay the wedding thirty minutes, giving the guests time to arrive. At 8:25 A.M., exactly five minutes before they were to be married, a temple worker rushed in, took their "time only" tags off, and replaced them with new tags which said "sealing." The so desired clearance had been received from the First Presidency only moments before.

Most in the Salt Lake area would probably consider that snowstorm just another act of nature. One couple, however, learned that fasting and prayer for a righteous desire can produce miracles.

More Things Are Wrought by Prayer

ALFRED, LORD TENNYSON

More things are wrought by prayer
Than this world dreams of. Wherefore, let thy voice
Rise like a fountain for me night and day.
For what are men better than sheep or goats
That nourish a blind life within the brain,
If, knowing God, they lift not hands of prayer
Both for themselves and those who call them friends?
For so the whole round earth is every way
Bound by gold chains about the feet of God.

His Eyes Will Be Healed

JANE D. BRADY

I could tell that Sam was paying attention. We were reading Alma, chapter 34 while sitting around the kitchen table. Sure, he listened intently to the Book of Mormon battle scenes and he seemed to pay attention better when we had him read every tenth verse or so, but kids' minds do wander. Still, I remember distinctly the feeling I had as we read—a "he's listening" impression.

We had made a goal to finish reading the Book of Mormon before Sam's baptism in the summer of 1998. To help the kids (and us) stay motivated we got one of those charts that says "I Have Read the Book of Mormon" with several squares in each letter of the saying to signify each individual chapter. The kids were excited to mark off each square. Thanks to that, and to our sly idea of feeding them some kind of little treat right before bed, they would sit quietly at the kitchen table and listen while they munched. At least they were quiet and they sat still. Who could say if they were really listening, really hearing?

The goal was a good one, we knew that. Certainly nothing *bad* could come from following a commandment, from inviting the Spirit into our home every day. But when children are young, it is difficult to determine what kind of effect the scriptures are having on them. It felt more like we *weren't doing something wrong* than it felt like we were doing something right, if you know what I mean.

Let me remind you of some of the words comprising Alma 34:

> Therefore may God grant unto you, my brethren, that ye may begin to exercise your faith unto repentance, that ye begin to call upon his holy name, that he would have mercy upon you;
>
> Yea, cry unto him for mercy; for he is mighty to save.
>
> Yea, humble yourselves, and continue in prayer unto him.

Cry unto him when ye are in your fields, yea, over all your flocks.

Cry unto him in your houses, yea, over all your household, both morning, mid-day, and evening.

"Why are they crying?" McKenna asked.

"They're not," Sam answered. "He's talking about praying. He's saying when you should pray."

"When *should* you pray?" she asked. (Yep, she's four.)

"Everywhere!" Sam said, a little impatient at this point.

Cry unto him over the crops of your fields, that ye may prosper in them.

Cry over the flocks of your fields, that they may increase.

But this is not all; ye must pour out your souls in your closets, and your secret places, and in your wilderness.

Yea, and when you do not cry unto the Lord, let your hearts be full, drawn out in prayer unto him continually for your welfare, and also for the welfare of those who are around you.

"Could I pray for a Nintendo 64?" Sam wanted to know.

"What do you think?" Ken responded. (You can tell he's had experience with these kinds of questions.)

"Why not? He says to pray about the flocks, about things they want. I want an N-64."

"Prayer *is* about things that you want, but things that you want which are good. Things that God wants you to have and knows are best for you," Ken responded.

"I don't see what's wrong with wanting an N-64. I don't see how that wouldn't be best for me."

"That's the point, though; we *don't* always see what's best for us, but God always does. He always knows."

Yet Sam had a good point. Weren't there things that *I* wanted enough to hope for, even pray and plead for, not caring what was best for me, just focusing on my deeply felt need? I thought about that as Ken read the rest of the chapter. Then, in verse 38 my answer seemed to come:

> That ye contend no more against the Holy Ghost, but that ye receive it, and take upon you the name of Christ; that ye humble yourselves even to the dust, and worship God, in whatsoever place ye may be in, in spirit and in truth; and that ye live in thanksgiving daily, for the many mercies and blessings which he doth bestow upon you.

It was months later before I remembered that particular evening around the dinner table, our discussion of Alma 34, and the distinct feeling I'd had that Sam had been listening.

> Prayer is the act by which the will of the Father and the will of the child are brought into correspondence with each other. (Bible Dictionary, "Prayer")

Sam had a problem. He'd been playing a game on the computer and his eyes were beginning to hurt. He so wanted to keep playing that he kept going until the pain became unbearable. At that point he panicked. In his seven-year-old mind he imagined the worst. Would the pain ever stop? Was he going blind? Sam decided this emergency was exactly the kind of thing he should pray about. Alone in the study he folded his arms and prayed for the pain to stop. He believed in God. He knew God was powerful. He knew that God could stop the pain; he had faith in that. So he prayed and prayed, and then he said amen.

Nothing changed.

He waited for a few minutes (a long time for him) and still nothing happened. If anything, the pain was getting worse. He squeezed his eyes as tightly as he could but he couldn't shut out the pain.

> The object of prayer is not to change the will of God, but to secure for ourselves and for others blessings that God is already willing to grant, but that are made conditional on our asking for them. (Bible Dictionary, "Prayer")

So far Sam's story wasn't too surprising to me. I know the goodness in Sam's soul. I know he tries to do what is right. What surprised me was what came next: a giant leap of faith, so big that many adults never take it. Sam realized that his prayer had been wrong. He had been *telling* God what to do instead of *asking* Him what to do. He started over. This time he explained his problem to God and then told Him he would do whatever He said. He wanted the pain to stop and would do whatever it took, even if it meant to stop playing his game—something he really didn't want to do. Even if it meant coming to tell me, which surely meant no more computer games. Sam remembers saying amen and sitting there for a moment with his arms folded, just sitting quietly and waiting. Then came, strongly, into his heart, the message, "Tell your mom. She'll know what to do."

> Blessings require some work or effort on our part before we can obtain them. (Bible Dictionary, "Prayer")

When Sam came to me I knew immediately that his problem was serious. He was choked up, he even had a difficult time getting the words out. Finally he communicated to me that his eyes hurt and that he was very worried about them. Knowing how seldom Sam complains, I figured they really were stinging. I knew he had been reading all morning and since then had been playing on the computer, so I assumed his eyes were just tired, aching from overuse. At first I thought I'd tell him to rest them for a while, that he should just lie down with his eyes closed and I would put a cool, moist cloth over them. But as soon as I thought that, I knew it wasn't right. I knew Sam needed me. I decided to drop off the little girls at a friend's house to play, and then Sam and I went alone to the doctor's office. Although I wasn't as worried as Sam, I wanted to take him seriously. I wanted to take care of him completely.

> Prayer is a form of work, and is an appointed means for obtaining the highest of all blessings. (Bible Dictionary, "Prayer")

Though the doctor was busy, the nurse saw us immediately. She could tell, as I could, that Sam was upset, deeply concerned. She was very gentle and attentive to him. She looked carefully into his eyes. She had him read the eye chart. Then she asked him questions about what he had been doing all day. Coming to the same conclusion that I had, she told him it was important to do all kinds of different things with his eyes—from big things like catching a ball to small things like reading a book. Now that his eyes were overtired from too much strain he'd need to rest them for a long while. She gave him some drops to help him to feel better. And Sam really did feel better. He knew he wasn't going to go blind or die. He knew that I loved him. He knew that God had heard him.

On the way home Sam explained to me all that had happened. He told me about his two prayers and the big change in between. He said he knew he was going to be all right now.

> There are many instances of Jesus healing the blind. Indeed, part of his mission as foretold by Isaiah included "recovering of sight to the blind." . . . In addition to the healing of physical blindness, the mission of Jesus included curing blindness to the things of the spirit. He made an application of this in John 9:5 when, in conjunction with healing the man born blind, he declared that he (Jesus) was "the light of the world." (Bible Dictionary, "Blindness")

> The Light of Christ will lead the honest soul who "hearkeneth to the voice" to find the tru[lth]. (Bible Dictionary, "Light of Christ")

I imagine Sam, eighteen years old, with some problem, some difficulty that seems as if it will never go away. I can believe that he would pray about it. We've prayed with him since the day he was born. We've brought him to church. We've tried to teach him the right things. And who doesn't pray in a crisis? Who doesn't plead with God to make it all go away? What I hope with all of my heart is that Sam will remember the scriptures that we've read with him and remember the examples of the prophets. I hope he will pray, not for his own will but for God's will to be done. Because if he does, his eyes will be healed, and one day they will open upon the face of God.

The Answer Was No

ANNE OSBORN POELMAN

Having completed my medical training at Stanford University (thirteen years of relentless, highly competitive education after high school), and being a relatively new member of the Church, I left California for my first real job: Instructor of Radiology at the University of Utah School of Medicine.

I looked forward to enjoying the single social scene in Utah. Everyone had warned me that the ratio of single men to single women in Salt Lake City was far from promising. But compared to Palo Alto, it seemed like a veritable Promised Land. In California I had known almost no worthy, tithe-paying, temple-going, single Latter-day Saint men in their thirties. Or forties. Or (gulp) even their fifties.

After arriving in Salt Lake City I dated what seemed like nearly every eligible bachelor between Logan and Springville, Maine to Montana. Enduring innumerable dates and even some euphemistically termed "Special Interest" events seemed a small price to pay for the possibility of an eternal companionship and the blessing of celestial marriage.

It didn't happen.

Thirty-one passed in a flash. Thirty-two. Thirty-five. The years inexorably rolled by. Good ones. Lonely ones. Despite my best intentions, I still sometimes nagged the Lord. And I almost—but not quite—got married.

I finally decided that one very nice, soft-spoken widower came reasonably close to what I thought was desirable in an eternal companion. He was considerably older than I, but from the eternal perspective that really doesn't count for much, does it? When he asked me to marry him, I hesitated only because I hadn't received the strong spiritual confirmation that had accompanied other truly crucial decisions in my life.

I put him off. Frustrated, he began pressing for an answer. So, in fasting and prayer, I finally went to the temple. After the session was finished I sat in the celestial room for what seemed like hours, entreating the Lord to reveal his will. Should my answer be "yes," "no," or perhaps "I'm still not sure"?

Cosmic silence.

I had temporarily forgotten a fundamental lesson from the scriptures that I had learned years before as an investigator. As if through a still, small voice this scripture came to mind: "Behold, you have not understood; you have supposed that I would give it unto you, when you took not thought save it was to ask me.

"But, behold, I say unto you, that you must study it out in your mind; then you must ask me if it be right, and if it is right I will cause that your bosom shall burn within you; therefore, you shall feel that it is right" (D&C 9:8).

Impatient, I finally said to the Lord, "Well, I've made up my mind. I'm going to do it. I'm going to marry Brother _____. If I'm right, please let me feel peace about it. And if I'm not, *please* let me know."

The ensuing reply was a single firm but powerful mental "*No!*" The impression was so strong it almost seemed auditory. Startled at the strength of the unexpected answer, I looked up and said out loud, "*What?*" Gently shushed by a nearby temple worker, I repeated the inquiry and received the same impression.

I'm chagrined and embarrassed to admit it, but I didn't actually believe the answer. I thought my vivid imagination was working overtime. I left the temple intending to accept the proposal. Still somewhat uncertain about my decision, I dismissed my nagging anxieties. I temporarily succeeded in suppressing the uncomfortable feeling that something wasn't quite right. But however much I tried, those uncomfortable sensations would not disappear completely.

The afternoon of the next day, a bright and beautiful Sabbath, I was quietly reading when someone knocked at the front door. I peeked out the window and was surprised to see one of the priesthood leaders in our stake standing on the doorstep. He told me he was out walking in the neighborhood and thought he'd drop by "just to see how I was doing."

It was odd. Definitely odd. I had seen his wife out walking briskly on many occasions, but never her husband. This good man is a modest, rather diffident person. So when he came in and sat down in the living room, he was understandably somewhat uncomfortable and ill at ease.

After a few halting, desultory comments, he finally cleared his throat and came to the point. "I suppose I'd better tell you why I came by," he began with some hesitation. "Last night I just couldn't get to sleep. So after tossing and turning for a while I finally gave up. I went downstairs into the study to read and ponder the scriptures. After a while I began meditating, then praying, pouring my heart out to the Lord in gratitude for his mercy and blessings. At that moment I think I felt closer to the Lord than at any other time in my life. The veil seemed so thin it was as though I could almost reach through it."

He paused at the vivid memory, then continued, "The Lord made some things known to me, personal things about some events that would take place in my life later on. Then at the end of my prayer, something quite unusual happened. I began to think about you. And I had the unmistakable impression that you were facing a critical decision in your life. I wasn't told what it was. No details. But what I *was* told by the Spirit is that you were about to make the wrong choice. Whatever that is," he smiled almost apologetically, "you're supposed to say no!"

I was stunned. How could he possibly have known?

"Well, actually . . . I *am* in a real quandary about something very important," I admitted. Then I corrected myself, "I mean I *was* in a quandary. I was going to say 'yes' when I know I should say 'no.' Not to anything bad," I added hastily. "Now I know what I need to do."

So I turned down the proposal. But it would be years before I would know how right that decision was.

I learned an important lesson from that experience. When we plead with the Lord for help, *the answer to our prayers often comes through another individual.* It has been said that answers to prayer usually don't come down through the roof but they do come knocking on the door! The corollary is that we should strive to be spiritually in tune so that, should he choose, the Lord can use us to bless the lives of others.

THE *Power* OF THE *Word*

"A Joy Which Is Unspeakable"

Neal E. Lambert

Our daughter had been studying the Beethoven Fourth Piano Concerto and was scheduled to perform it as part of an important competition in Colorado. The history of that study was not always smooth. Earlier that year we had visited Lara at a summer music camp and attended a master class where she was to play the first movement of the concerto before a group of fellow students. In such a class the instructor—in this case a remarkably demanding teacher—usually critiques and comments as the student plays, stopping, coaching, and generally questioning and guiding the performance. This particular concerto opens with the piano alone and without the orchestra, in an extraordinary announcement of the theme, which is then followed by a response from the full orchestra. The teacher had announced to our daughter, "When you play that first chord, everyone will know what that performance will mean," and then she asked, "So what do you want to do with this piece? What is it about?" The Beethoven Fourth Piano Concerto is not exactly program music; it is not about a cloudburst or the ocean or a sunset. So the unexpected question was obviously unsettling to the poor girl at the piano who had, with this piece at least, been more concerned with notes than with ideas. But the teacher was unsympathetic and insistent, and kept pressing the question before allowing the performance to go on. Unable to satisfy her instructor, Lara, now almost in tears, could hardly play at all for the rest of the class, and at the end of her portion of the master class escaped to the back of the room in deep disappointment.

Many months of practice later, she was now in Colorado, preparing to play that same concerto in competition with some of the best young pianists from the Western United States. As one can easily imagine, such a competition is an extraordinarily intense environment: nervous performers are pacing back and forth, some with gloves on their precious hands, waiting their turn before the judges; others are with teachers giving passionate, whispered, last-minute instructions; there are self-congratulatory, budding prima-donnas talking about the performance they are about to give; and, above all, are the scales, the runs, and the thunderous chords emanating from the warm-up rooms where the musicians work over shaky passages and loosen their fingers as they try to get the adrenaline under control. Everyone's attention is tied to the concert hall where, halfway back, the three judges, alone in the otherwise empty hall, await the next performer. The rooms, the halls, and above all the performance auditorium are electric with the intensity of the moment.

This is the environment in which Lara was to perform. A half an hour or so before her scheduled appearance, she asked for a priesthood blessing of peace. And then her mother and I left her alone in the warm-up room and made our way to the auditorium and the back row where a few family members and friends were allowed to quietly observe the proceedings.

At the scheduled time, her name was announced, Lara stepped onto the stage, and, with her sister at the accompanying piano, took her place at the keyboard of the concert grand. The judges said nothing, just nodded the go-ahead. But then, Lara didn't play. Instead of beginning the concerto, she just sat at the piano for what seemed to me like an eternity, even though it couldn't have been more than fifteen or twenty seconds. Finally— slowly and deliberately—she raised her hands to the keyboard, and that first chord rose from the piano as if by magic. Then the notes of the opening theme filled the hall, and as the accompanying piano followed with the orchestral response, I had the sense that something truly remarkable was happening. As the concerto continued, that feeling grew, and a sense of peace and joy that was almost palpable filled the auditorium. I could see the judges listening and writing their comments, but as the music went on, they wrote less and less and listened more and more to what was developing in the music. Eventually, they seemed to quit writing altogether; they put their pencils down, leaned back, and just listened with obvious pleasure. I knew they felt what we were feeling—the remarkable spirit of this piece.

After the glorious finale, Lara left the stage, and we hurried quickly to the foyer to meet her. She was smiling and obviously happy about what had just happened. We were deeply pleased as well. After the hugs and kisses and congratulations, I asked Lara about those suspenseful seconds of contemplation before she began to play. And then she told us of her remarkable experience as she waited for her turn to perform.

When we left her in the warm-up room before the performance, she was about to continue to rehearse some difficult sections of the concerto, but, knowing the benefit at this point would be minimal, she decided instead to read her scriptures. The Book of Mormon has very little to say about either Beethoven or playing the piano. So this was simply a continuation of a practice rooted in family experience and personal habit, a habit of daily scripture reading. She just opened the pages where the yellow ribbon marked her stopping point from the day before, Helaman, chapter 5. This is the account of two great missionaries, Lehi and Nephi, their imprisonment, their deliverance, and the miraculous bestowal of the Holy Ghost upon them and the people around them. As Lara read, she came to verse 44: "And Nephi and Lehi were in the midst of them; yea, they were encircled about; yea, they were as if in the midst of a flaming fire, yet it did harm them not, neither did it take hold upon the walls of the prison; and they were filled with *that joy which is unspeakable and full of glory*" (emphasis added). "That's it!" Lara said. "That is what this concerto is all about—'that joy which is unspeakable and full of glory!'" Those words from the Book of Mormon were the answer that she didn't have earlier that summer; they articulated for her the "meaning" of that concerto. And that was what she was thinking about in the seconds before she performed as she bowed her head and let those words from the Book of Mormon pass through her mind; and that was what we all felt as she played—a "joy which is unspeakable and full of glory!"

The Time My Father Ripped Up the Book of Mormon

James H. Fedor

My father's unique outlook on the gospel and life in general was evident the very first time the missionaries knocked on our door over thirty-five years ago in inner city Cleveland. When the two young Elders introduced themselves as representatives of The Church of Jesus Christ of Latter-day Saints, my father was amazed at the church with such a long name and replied, "The church of *what?*" When the missionaries rejoined that the Church was commonly referred to as the Mormon Church, my father then said, "Oh, I know who you are *now*—you're the grasshopper people!"

In response to the missionaries' puzzled looks, my dad explained, "I just saw your movie about that guy who took his church out west in the wagons and the grasshoppers were eating up all your crops. And then he prayed for help and God sent thousands of seagulls to eat up all the grasshoppers!"

The missionaries were surprised that Dad was acquainted with their story. My father admitted, "You know, if that really happened, that was a *miracle!*"

The Elders smiled between themselves and assured my father that it was indeed a miracle and asked him if he'd like to know more. And the rest, as they say, is now a part of my Mormon family history.

I was five at the time, and mostly what I remember is the missionaries' hats and suits, the filmstrips that they would project onto the wall in our living room, and flannel boards with little word strips and pictures that never seemed to stick.

The Elders gave to my parents copies of a book they said was the word of God, and challenged them to read a prescribed number of pages each week. My father eagerly took up the challenge, intent to prove the book was false. Each week he would read his one hundred pages, and when the missionaries would ask him what he thought of it, he would reply that he hadn't "found anything wrong with it *yet.*"

After a month and a half my father finished the last page of the Book of Mormon and told my mother that he could find nothing in this book that wasn't true. My parents were baptized a few weeks later.

Dad now reveres that book that dated a new era of his life. He has read it many, many times. And because he loved it so much, one spring he ripped it up.

My father was a laborer for a division of General Motors for more than thirty years. He put in a lot of time at the huge factory that was over half a mile long. He realized that during the course of a normal day many valuable moments would come that could be put to good use studying the gospel if he would just plan ahead. He determined to use his lunch hour, break time, and waiting periods to get more intimate with the book that had changed his faith and his life.

The only problem was that he couldn't always carry around with him a book of more than five hundred pages. In my mind, the solution my father came up with bordered on genius. He took an old, dog-eared copy of the Book of Mormon and ripped off its brown simulated-leather cover and binding until just a stack of pages remained. Each morning before he went to work, Dad would take four or five pages and fold them up to fit into his shirt pocket. During his free moments at work he would then take out his precious pages and read and reread them at least three or four times. As he left work he would leave those pages in his locker.

Over the course of the next few months the stack of pages of the Book of Mormon at home would dwindle as he consumed them in those spare moments someone has called "the gold dust of time." Likewise, at the end of each work day, the reassembled stack of pages would grow higher in his locker. And in my father's heart there also grew a stronger and stronger love for and commitment to the gospel of Jesus Christ and the book which revealed it to him so clearly. That spring my father reread the Book of Mormon three or four times.

My father has taught me many lessons in my life but perhaps none was taught so simply and profoundly as when he creatively made time for a thing that really mattered.

I have used his reading technique on a few books myself when I wanted to utilize my time better and when I thought the book was worthy of assimilation in such an intimate way. It was Francis Bacon who said, "Some books are to be tasted, others to be swallowed, and some few to be chewed and digested." And, following in Dad's footsteps, I would add that some books are good enough to be ripped up and carried in one's pocket to be read over and over again.

Now when I go into the homes of the Saints and see old, inexpensive copies of the Book of Mormon collecting dust on shelves, I think of my father's example and how those old copies could be "feasted upon" by ripping them up. It goes without saying that this is a holy book and should be treated with respect. I am firmly convinced, though, that the very finest way to respect the word of God is to rewrite it onto "the fleshy tables" of our hearts. I know of a good way to do that now—my father's way.

Miracles and Family Scripture Study

ELAINE CANNON

Adam and Eve "made all things known unto their sons and their daughters" (Moses 5:12). So did Father Lehi. King Benjamin was diligent in this, and all the prophets in our day have so counseled. Joseph Smith said, "I teach them correct principles and they govern themselves." It remains for parents in our day to follow their inspired leaders, especially to see to it that correct principles are taught so that their children have enough knowledge to govern their own decisions.

These are the flat facts behind why Jim and I started a Sunday scripture read-aloud even though the children were barely able to read. We knew that our posterity should experience the sweet and saving truths of the gospel for themselves by searching the word with their own senses—seeing, hearing, speaking the word out loud. We made some personal sacrifice in groceries so that each one had a set of scriptures, except the toddler, who had a Golden Book of Jesus from which he took a turn "reading."

It was perhaps the best gift we gave our children through all the years.

Jim introduced us to this tradition by telling us a tender story from his Hawaiian mission days. A worn Bible was his visual aid. In a country town on the island of Maui, a young boy lay close to death with a dangerously high fever. The doctor had done everything he knew. There were no life-saving miracle antibiotics at that time. The Elders had been called in to administer a healing blessing. Jim explained to our family, "Before the anointing, I asked the boy if he knew about Jesus. He nodded his head weakly without opening his eyes. Then I put this Bible on his chest and laid his hand on it so he could feel it. I told him this was the sacred book that described all about Jesus and the good things He did—how He placed His hands on sick people and made them well. I read out loud from Mark 9 (we all opened our Bibles to Mark 9) where it is recorded that a father brought his son to Jesus to be healed from a terrible illness. The scripture says: 'Jesus said unto him, If thou canst believe, all things are possible to him that believeth. And straightway the father of the child cried out, and said with tears, Lord, I believe; help thou my unbelief' (Mark 9:23–24).

"I wasn't certain that this sick boy was well enough or trained sufficiently to understand what I was saying," Jim related, "but we went ahead and gave him the anointing and sealing ordinance. When I lifted my hands from his head and reached to take my Bible from his chest, the boy tightened his grip around the book. He would not let it go. And we left.

"Two days later we visited with the family again about the boy's condition. They reported that he was much improved. He had hugged that Bible all night. The family felt sorry that the Bible got soaked from the boy's incredible perspiration as the fever finally broke. But that book became even more valuable to me because of the boy's faith."

Jim flipped the pages to show our children the stained cover and sheets, allowing each child to handle his Bible. It had a profound effect on them.

During every scripture session, each member of our family took a turn reading a few verses from the selected scripture. Not to be left out, the toddler very soberly "read" a brief bit of baby jargon from his picture book. Of course, we flooded him with compliments. Then one day an amazing thing happened. He insisted on reading from my Bible. Apparently he had noticed how the siblings, who were beginning readers, moved a finger across the printed lines. This was to help them keep their place. Sitting on my lap, Tony put his tiny finger on the text in my Bible. When it was his turn to "read" he babbled his nonsense. Suddenly he said, "Jesus!" and pointed to that sacred name in print. Maybe he recognized the letters he had seen in his baby book. Surely something clicked in his mind. Whatever else it was to this child not yet two years old, he miraculously had caught on to reading, which was about symbols the mind recognized to stir the soul. And "Jesus" was his first experience with recognizing truth through the scriptures!

It was a high moment, a memory repeated for our youngest child as he grew up and was ordained a deacon, honored at a missionary farewell, a wedding shower, and then, too soon, a funeral when he was only forty-two and the father of three. Tony's epitaph was one of his favorite scriptures, and surely appropriate for him as a competing Boston Marathon runner: "Thy word is a lamp unto my feet, and a light unto my path" (Psalm 119:105).

"It's Not a Problem Anymore"

BRENT L. TOP

Bishops and mission presidents often have the opportunity to see the power of the Lord's revealed word firsthand. One mission president shared with me his astonishment at the responsibility that he had as a mission president. He was surprised that so little of his time was spent on missionary work. Most of it was used up in solving problems, hearing confessions, listening to the discouraged, avoiding and trying to break up companionship problems, and attempting to keep Elders and Sisters and couples together.

On one occasion he thought, *How in the world am I going to be able to get this mission to do the things it needs to do?* He decided that he would institute throughout the mission a one-month program of serious study of the Book of Mormon and ask the Elders and Sisters and couples in the mission to suspend all interviews with the mission president during that period. He asked every missionary to seriously study the Book of Mormon that month, to study the scriptures carefully each day, not just reading but feasting, as Nephi said (see 2 Nephi 31:20).

At the end of the month he resumed his schedule of problem-solving and interviewing. He called the first Elder in and said, "Well, Elder, what's the problem that we need to talk to you about?" The missionary said, "Well, President, it's not a problem anymore." The next Elder came in, and in answer to the president's question replied, "I can't remember what the problem is." One after another the experience was the same.

Problems that once seemed so insurmountable had been solved. The missionaries no longer needed to rely on the mission president, for they found their own answers in the scriptures and had allowed the Spirit to touch their lives.

"Victoria Doesn't Believe"

Angie T. Hinckley

While he was in law school my husband's time during the week was mostly taken up with classes and studying, but he made an effort to read with our two preschoolers, Caroline and Rob, right after dinner before returning to his studies. They all "read" together from their own set of illustrated scripture stories of the standard works of the Church. The children enjoyed this time with their father, and they quickly made it through all the books, but I didn't realize the impact it was having until almost a year later.

We were living in Las Vegas across the street from a wonderful Catholic family who had a young daughter close to the ages of our own children. One day while they were playing together in our home, our son Rob came running into the kitchen anxiously saying, "Mom, where are the books, Victoria doesn't believe." It took me a minute to realize that my preschoolers were having a religious discussion with their young neighbor. Rob was obviously concerned over his friend's lack of understanding, but seemed sure that his "scriptures" would set her straight. Armed with the Book of Mormon, the Doctrine and Covenants, and Bible scripture stories he went back to the playroom. I walked past the room a time or two and caught part of a three-degrees-of-glory discussion.

Victoria left soon afterwards. I asked my children how it had gone, and Rob expressed his concern that she still did not believe. We speculated that her lack of faith might be due to her not knowing all the scriptures. Caroline immediately asked if we should let her borrow ours.

I realized from this experience of watching my children's spontaneous "bearing of testimony" to their friend that the responsibility of the covenant "to bear this ministry" will flow naturally from a desire to share our understanding of a loving Father. Fortified with a firm faith in a loving and all-knowing Heavenly Father, our children will be prepared to faithfully endure and confidently trust, even when faced with difficult times.

$\mathscr{A}$ Torn Page

Robert E. Wells

Two missionaries were walking home in the blinding, hot noonday sun of Mexico. Most people were off the street, sheltered inside and ready for a siesta until the day cooled off. The cobblestone street was irregular to walk on but was in better condition than the broken sidewalk. They rounded a corner of the narrow street, and there in front of them—lying on the hard cobblestones, belly up, spread-eagled in the sun, flies buzzing around him—was a pitiful drunk who had passed out.

The two Elders looked around—not a person in sight. All doors were closed, all windows shuttered against the heat. There was a tree growing out of the sidewalk close by, so they picked the drunk up between the two of them and lugged him into the shade. They rolled him over on his side and rested his head on his arm so he looked a little more presentable.

As the two started to leave, they looked around once more to see if anyone wanted to claim the derelict. A call came from across the street through the shutters of a window. "Thank you for pulling him out of the street. That was a thoughtful thing to do." They walked towards the voice and asked, "Do you know which house he belongs in?" The lady inside said no, she had never seen him before but was glad he was not in front of her house anymore, and thanked them again.

Then she said something strange. "By the way, maybe you could help my son. Just a moment. I'll open the door." They thought she might have a drunk son. Such was not the case. She took them inside the house to where her university student son was studying.

"Son, maybe these young men can help you with that paper you found." Without a word he searched through the papers on his desk until he found it. It was a single page of double-column print that had been torn from a book. He showed it to the Elders. "I found this in the street about a block from here. I have read both sides. It seems somehow familiar. It is religious, but I don't think it is from the Bible. Do you know where this comes from?" The Elders smiled, and one of them opened a new Book of Mormon he was carrying to the same page, put the torn page in it, and closed the book. He then gave both back to the young man, saying, "It is from the Book of Mormon, a book about Christ written by ancient Christian prophets living here in the Americas. We can tell you all about this book, where it came from, and how it was translated to English and Spanish by the power of God." The mother and her son both joined the Church.

Just as President McKay told us "every member a missionary" and President Kimball reminded us to lengthen our stride and to quicken our step in doing missionary work, so President Benson set fire to our missionary enthusiasm by telling us to all take part in flooding the world with copies of the Book of Mormon.

President Benson quoted from the Doctrine and Covenants and warned us that we would continue to be under condemnation if we did not become more involved in placing this great and powerful book in the hands of all our friends, neighbors, acquaintances, and relatives: "Your minds in times past have been darkened because of unbelief, and because you have treated lightly the things you have received. . . . And [you] shall remain under this condemnation until [you] repent and remember the new covenant, even the Book of Mormon" (D&C 84:54, 57). "I will forgive you of your sins with this commandment—that you remain steadfast . . . in bearing testimony to all the world of those things which are communicated unto you [i.e., the Book of Mormon]" (D&C 84:61).

"Is This Really Doing Anybody Any Good?"

NEAL E. LAMBERT

As parents we may wonder sometimes whether the effort at regular scripture reading in the home is really worth the scrambles and troubles. Given the press of schedules and the sometimes conscious disinterest from people seated around the table, the task seems daunting. Every parent surely has experienced some of the mumbling grumbles and the studied boredom of teenagers, or the glassy-eyed unconsciousness of the nine- and ten-year-olds, or the distracting climbing up and down the furniture or the spoon pounding of the smallest toddlers. Surely we have each asked ourselves in these less-than-perfect family moments, "Is this really doing anybody any good?" Of course, in our hearts we know the answer even when that answer may never truly be evident until "after many days." But if we continue scripture reading in our homes, there will be times, perhaps years ahead, when a genuine surprise surfaces, a clear evidence of true spiritual penetration. I remember one such moment well.

We were sitting in a family council in the living room of a small house in central Massachusetts. Our little family, including our four youngest, had moved there during a sabbatical leave from Brigham Young University. My work was in Worcester, but the only accommodations we could afford for a family our size were in Dudley, one of the many small mill-towns scattered across the then less-than-prosperous countryside. The house was "different" in its arrangement, but we had accommodated ourselves to the one bathtub and sharing the half-bath with the washing machine. The unmistakably used furniture of the house still smelled of the nightclub that our landlord operated, from which the piano and couches had already seen considerable service.

Our little house was unusual, to say the least, but for our year away from home, it was doable.

Our family enjoyed many wonderful experiences together in New England, generally, and in the Worcester Ward in particular where we had an abundance of good times and good friends. Still, in the depth of that New England winter the anticipation of returning to our own comfortable home in Provo, Utah, was real. Before leaving the previous summer, our daughters had given last, longing looks at their bedrooms which they had just finished decorating. And during the intervening months they had talked more than once about having again closets and drawers for their own clothes, places for their pictures, shelves for their books, and enjoying again the friends and opportunities and comforts they had loved in the lives they left behind in Utah.

So our family council that January night was important and very serious. It concerned our return home. That day we had received a call from President Gordon B. Hinckley to serve for the next three years as mission president. We didn't yet know where, but we knew accepting the call would mean not returning to Provo next summer as we had planned. But our situation was more complicated than just postponing a return to our new house. We were in the middle of raising eight daughters, and our family expenses were at their highest point. Accepting the call might well mean having to sell our home. I explained as much to the family, so, as one might expect, the discussion was less than gleeful. As we talked over the possibilities and the implications for us, for our house—and for the bedrooms—I could see some chins quiver, and a few eyes brimmed with tears. Then our daughter Toni wiped her eyes and said, "Now I know how Laman and Lemuel felt. They just didn't want to leave their beautiful new home in Jerusalem."

There was a world of meaning in that response—for Toni, and for our family. It was clear that for her Laman and Lemuel were more than ciphers or story characters. They were real people in real-life situations. And those of us sitting there that night with Toni knew that she knew the record that told of *their* leaving home was true. Furthermore we knew that because the record was true, we would all, like Lehi and Nephi, "go and do," wherever and however the prophet called us. I don't know where Toni came to her testimony of Laman and Lemuel and Sam and Nephi and all the others in the Book of Mormon and the other scriptures. Whether or not it was in those seemingly futile mornings trying to do scriptures and cereal and sack lunches and carpool arrangements before the family shot out through all the doors to their schools and practices and appointments, I couldn't really say. Certainly seminary and Sunday School had a good deal to do with it. But what matters is this: that night in Massachusetts, Toni knew, and we knew, even in the face of difficult choices, what we must do, and what we would do. To start that night a practice of family scripture reading would have been too late. On the day when it was crucial, the scriptural familiarity was there, and our Lambert Liahona-guide worked for Toni and for us all.

Lessons Learned in the "Mole Hole"

ELAINE CANNON

We called the sunny room on our second floor the Mole Hole. It was the place where the women of the family (who outnumbered the men) became buried in projects like laundry duty, hair styling and drying, poster painting for school and church visuals, and family needs requiring the sewing machine. Great "girl talk" happened here, too. But one busy day (at the peak of my parenting years) this Mole Hole was the scene of a crushing blow to my self-esteem as the mother in a gospel-oriented family.

I sat at the sewing machine preoccupied with a rush job of stitching a skirt for a daughter who was experiencing her first season working away from home. Suddenly I realized her younger sister was leaning against the door frame watching me. When she noted my attention she flung these burning words at me, "Mom, why are you always sewing for Kiki and never for me?" I heard the sob before she disappeared.

I was stunned. Our uncomplaining young teenager was complaining. Our competent seamstress was being incompatible.

My martyr's day complex heightened.

My immediate reaction was to tangle my guiding finger with the sewing machine needle. The pain was severe and I matched it to her uneasy heart—which must have been uneasy and pained or she never would have blurted out such jealous words. She wouldn't dare question my motives so rudely. But she had dared! A teaching moment was at hand, if only I could think what to say.

My second reaction was just as automatic. I prayed, "Which of Heavenly Father's principles will help me now?"

I put my mind on seek and search. With which absolute from the word of God could I appease my beloved youngest daughter?

How could I help her to understand that, indeed, each disappointment in life has a remedy in the scriptures.

Still praying, I went into her room, put an arm about her shoulders, and reminded her of Christ's parable of the prodigal son. The key players were the errant son, the jealous older brother, and the understanding father. Then I likened the biblical cast to our own family. I further explained that this was a type of the forgiving Heavenly Father shows us when we make mistakes.

"I am sewing for Kiki because she needs help right now. But—" I paused a moment— "do you have any idea how much I love you because I *don't* have to sew for you? Tired mother that I am, I am grateful you are one skilled seamstress and I am proud of you."

I went back to my sewing machine. In a few minutes she came to me with the idea that she could prepare a care package of goodies for her sister that could include the skirt I was stitching. Again I was thankful for the scriptures which had provided common ground for seeing, comprehending, and healing.

The truth is, that when you look for a scripture to solve a certain problem, you find so many wonderful thoughts on a variety of other subjects that hope wipes out worry.

Glimpses of Eternity

"The First Game That He Ever Saw Me Play"

Sterling W. Sill

Whether the accomplishment is athletic, occupational, spiritual, familial, social, political, or personal, it is one of the thrilling experiences of life to see any great human creation, formed in God's image and endowed with his attributes, function on the level of a champion. But no one ever does his best without some kind of a cheering section. It is an old truth that no one lives unto himself alone. A part of the winning football score belongs to the coach, some goes to the parents, and some belongs to the cheerleaders and the people who sit in the grandstands.

The story is told of a high school quarterback whose father died just before the school's most crucial game. The coach told this young man that he would be excused from drill and play. But this was not what the boy wanted. He was so definite in the expression of his desire to play that the coach finally agreed to let him start. All during the game he played far over his head. He passed and kicked and blocked and ran the ends like Superman. His spirit and courage inspired his teammates with an ability greater than their own. The resounding cheers from the bleachers added to the electrification and the team won a colossal victory.

As the players left the field, the coach put his arm around the young hero and said, "Bill, would you like to tell me about it? How could you play as you did under these circumstances?" The boy said, "Coach, what you may not know is that my father was blind, and this was the first game that he ever saw me play."

$\mathscr{I}$ Would Give All That I Am

MELVIN J. BALLARD

I know that no man or woman shall ever come to stand in the presence of our Father in Heaven, or be associated with the Lord Jesus Christ, who does not grow spiritually. Without spiritual growth we shall not be prepared to enter into the divine presence. I need the sacrament. I need to renew my covenant every week. I need the blessing that comes with and through it. . . . I bear witness to you that I know that the Lord lives. I know that He has made this sacrifice and this atonement. He has given me a foretaste of these things.

I recall an experience which I had, bearing witness to my soul of the reality of His death, of His crucifixion, and His resurrection, that I shall never forget. . . . Away on the Fort Peck Reservation where I was doing missionary work with some of our brethren, laboring among the Indians, seeking the Lord for light to decide certain matters pertaining to our work there, and receiving a witness from Him that we were doing things according to His will, I found myself one evening in the dreams of the night in that sacred building, the temple. After a season of prayer and rejoicing I was informed that I should have the privilege of entering into one of those rooms to meet a glorious Personage, and, as I entered the door, I saw, seated on a raised platform, the most glorious Being my eyes have ever beheld or that I ever conceived existed in all the eternal worlds. As I approached to be introduced, he arose and stepped towards me with extended arms, and he smiled as he softly spoke my name. If I shall live to be a million years old, I shall never forget that smile. He took me into his arms and kissed me, pressed me to his bosom, and blessed me, until the marrow of my bones seemed to melt! When he had finished, I fell at his feet, and, as I bathed them with my tears and kisses, I saw the prints of the nails in the feet of the Redeemer of the world. The feeling that I had in the presence of Him who hath all things in His hands, to have His love, His affection, and His blessing was such that if I ever can receive that of which I had but a foretaste, I would give all that I am, all that I ever hope to be to feel what I then felt!

Go to the sacrament table. Ah, that is a blessed privilege that I now rejoice in, and I would be ashamed, I know, as I felt then, to stand in His presence and try to offer any apology or any excuse for not having kept His commandments and honored Him by bearing witness, before the Father and before men, that I believe in Him, and that I take upon me His blessed name, and that I live by and through Him spiritually.

Mirrors of Eternity

SHELDON L. ANDERSON

As newly man and wife, we stood
Between opposing mirrors,
And saw our endless images
Reflect eternal years.

It's not just for this life, my dear,
Or till we pass death's door.
I'll love you till the end of time,
And then, I'll love you more.

And when I think that you are mine
For all eternity,
I cannot hold the thought. The joy
Becomes too much for me.

Forever may I find the ways
To speak my thankfulness
That in the sealing room this morning,
You responded, "Yes."

Higher Authority

HUGH B. BROWN

I was on leave in 1916, staying at the Regent Palace hotel in London, just off Piccadilly. A messenger came who said, "You are wanted at a certain hospital." I had become accustomed to being called upon for favors from the men, because of the office I held; and as I received this message I thought "Some boy who is ill wants a leave, wants to return home to recuperate. He is sending for me with a request that I exercise my authority in his behalf." And rather proudly I took my cap and my crop, called a taxi, and went to the hospital; and as I went I thought, "It is a great thing to be an officer in the King's army; it is a great thing to be able to do something for someone else, because of the mark on the shoulder or the cuff of the uniform."

I went rather proudly in the thought that I might be able to do something for someone because I was an officer of the King. I went into the hospital and was ushered into a little room; and there I saw a former Sunday School student of mine, one whom I had taught in the intermediate departments of the Sunday School in Canada years before. This boy was very sick. He reached out a trembling hand. He did not address me by my military title, but said, in a weakened voice, "Brother Brown, I sent for you because the doctor says I must die. You know I have a widowed mother out in Canada; you know she needs me. I sent to ask if you will exercise your authority in my behalf, administer to me, ask God to save my life."

When he asked me to exercise my authority, there suddenly dawned upon me, for I had temporarily seemingly forgotten, that I held an authority that was not to be known by the uniform I wore, that I held an authority that would enable me, if properly exercised, to ask favors, not of the King of England, not of the general in command of the army, for under these circumstances they were helpless, but an authority which enabled me to ask of God a favor for this boy; and in humility I knelt by the side of that boy's cot and exercised the authority of the Holy Priesthood. I humbly prayed God to spare his life for his widowed mother. God was good enough to hear my prayer, and he answered it.

I went into that hospital a proud British officer; I came out a humble Mormon elder.

"What Are You Going to Be?"

Elaine Cannon

Children have unusual ways of reminding us of some significant things, haven't they? They can even make grown men think, as I learned one day.

A little boy came clomping down the sidewalk in front of our house in his father's shoes; a tie was looped about his neck, and a man-size belt buckled tightly about his small waist dragged behind him like a tail. A kindly gentleman smiled at the child and asked, "Well, and what are you going to be when you grow up?"

"I'm going to be a daddy," said the boy quickly, flipping the tie. "See?" Then he looked up at the older man and asked the thought-provoking question, "What are you going to be when you grow up?"

The man was startled by such a precocious response, and it caused him to stretch his mind into eternity. After all, that was about the only place he had left to go. And in that context he had to admit to himself that, indeed, he still had some growing to do.

"I'm going to be a father," he solemnly said.

And commitment was born of that comment.

A man doesn't usually dream of becoming a heavenly schoolteacher or a heavenly engineer or a heavenly land developer, let alone a heavenly father. Many hard-working men, if they think about life after death at all, have a comfortable view of a proverbial pink cloud and an eternity of lounging to the music of harpists—or something like that.

Our neighbor knew better than that. The boy's question reminded that grown man about eternity—about life forever, standing at the head of his own chain of descendants in the presence of God, our Father in Heaven.

Realizing that possibility would make a man think; and it suggests some growing up in a dramatic way, doesn't it? We will need to remember and practice the supreme example of the Savior, who said, "What manner of men ought ye to be? Verily I say unto you, even as I am" (3 Nephi 27:27).

Isn't it interesting that of all the titles of honor and admiration that could be given him, God himself chose to be called simply Father? Since we are in training in life to become like God, our neighbor's answer to the little boy's question was a good one. We are in eternity now, and we are rapidly becoming what we are going to be.

*B*rent

BETTE S. MOLGARD

My parents met Max and Gwen Higginson on December 21, 1953, in the St. Alphonsus Hospital in Boise, Idaho. It was an important date for both couples. That day Gwen gave birth to a son, and my mother had me. They still keep in touch.

Seven years after we were born, the Higginsons had a special Down's syndrome son named Brent. Brent seemed to bring a touch of heaven into their home. He had difficulty learning to speak, but even when he was tiny he made it known that he wanted to go inside the temple. Gwen says whenever they would have an opportunity to go through a session at a temple, they would make arrangements for someone to watch Brent. They would let him see the temple, explain to him that someone like a grandma would be taking care of him when they went there. He would cry, "No, me in—not grandma. Please, me in." They would tell him maybe he could go in some day, but he wasn't quite big enough yet.

Brent's eighth year came and went without baptism. There was no need. Bruce R. McConkie explains:

> When a child reaches the age at which he has sufficient mental, spiritual, and physical maturity to be held accountable before God for his acts, he is said to have arrived at the *years of accountability*. He then knows right from wrong and can exercise his agency to do good or evil. . . .
>
> . . . Children who develop normally become accountable "when eight years old" (D&C 68:27), and they are then subject to the law of baptism. Obviously if children or adults do not develop mentally to the point where they know right from wrong and have the normal intellect of an accountable person, they never arrive at the years of accountability no matter how many actual years they may live. Such persons, though they may be adults, are without the law, cannot

repent, are under no condemnation, "and unto such baptism availeth nothing." (Moroni 8:22.) Because they have no "understanding" it remains for the Lord "to do according as it is written" concerning them (D&C 29:48–50), that is, save them through the power of his redemptive sacrifice. (Moroni 8:22.) (*Mormon Doctrine* [Salt Lake City: Bookcraft, 1979], pp. 852–53)

When Brent was fourteen, his brother was serving a mission and kept writing about all of the people who were being baptized. Brent became adamant about his desire to be baptized. Following his baptism, Brent began asking when he could be a deacon. Soon he was a deacon, and many commented at how proud he was to pass the sacrament.

In 1985 the Boise Idaho Temple was completed, just two and a half miles from Brent's home. His parents, Max and Gwen, would go through the temple regularly. By this time, Brent was twenty-four and was old enough to take care of himself. He would say, "Don't worry, I be good" and then would sit in the temple waiting room, listening to tapes of scripture stories and following along in the books while his parents participated in a session. The waiting room, however, didn't satisfy his desire to go through the temple. He seemed to be the epitome of Elder Neal A. Maxwell's saying, "True disciples are meek but very determined" ("The Pathway of Discipleship," *Ensign*, September 1998, p. 8). Gwen said, "He launched a campaign that nearly drove the bishop crazy." Finally, toward the end of 1985, the bishop called them in and said, "I guess you know how much Brent desires to go through the temple. I've spoken with the stake president, and we have fasted and prayed about it. We agree that he can be made an elder and go through the temple for his endowment."

Brent received his own endowment and then desired to stand as proxy for others. After he had been several times, he was still struggling with a difficult part of the endowment. "I want to do that part better," he told his mom.

Gwen remembers explaining, "You know Brent, there is someone who can help you to do that." He quietly thought about it, then his face lit up as he understood. "I know," he responded, "Jesus can!"

That was on a Friday and Brent wouldn't be returning to the temple again until Tuesday. "Every time I saw him that entire weekend, he was on his knees asking for help," said Gwen. "The following Tuesday, it was like the heavens poured in blessings and Brent was able to do it."

Brent began going to the temple three times per week and now spends eight hours daily, five days per week acting as a proxy for fourteen endowments each week. A visiting authority recently said, "Brent Higginson has now endowed two stakes worth of souls, standing as proxy for over 4,800 endowments." Gwen smiles as she relates, "It's hard to talk Brent into going with us to visit our other children because he doesn't want to get behind in his temple work. We'll tell him about our intentions three weeks in advance so he has time to get used to the idea. He'll say, 'I know Mom, family first—but I love the temple!'"

What a blessing the temple has been to Brent, and what a blessing he has been in his thirty-nine years to his family, ward, stake, and his large circle of friends at the temple. He often spots them on shopping trips and runs to put his arms around them. As long as he is in the temple, nothing in his life is negative. Nothing of the world penetrates his days. When he sees any type of contention outside the temple, he doesn't understand. "Why would they do that? That wouldn't make Jesus happy." Brent Higginson has lived to be able to echo the words of our Savior, "In the world ye shall have tribulation: but be of good cheer; I have overcome the world" (John 16:33).

A Glimpse of Heaven

ROYDEN G. DERRICK

I had a glimpse of heaven recently. I was invited to seal a young couple from British Columbia in the Seattle Temple. We came together in one of the beautiful sealing rooms. For ten to twelve minutes I gave counsel to the bride and groom concerning some of the pitfalls and some of the joys and opportunities of marriage. Then I invited the groom to escort his bride to the far side of the altar, where she was to kneel, and asked him to kneel opposite her. As the bride walked to her place at the altar, I noticed that she was wearing a stunning white satin wedding dress covered with lace. It had a long, exquisite train. As she knelt at the altar she was radiant, confident, clean, sweet, and pure. The groom took his place at the altar and was equally impressive in a masculine way. I was ready to begin the ceremony when the bride's mother stood up, walked around the end of the altar, got down on her hands and knees, and began to straighten the train. First it was the satin cloth. Every wrinkle had to be straightened out. Then it was the lace. Again every wrinkle was to be smoothed out. Everything had to be perfect. It was the last finishing touch that a loving and caring and concerned mother could give to her daughter before she left to begin her own family. No peacock ever had a more beautiful train than this lovely bride had that day.

It took the mother three to four minutes to satisfy herself that everything was perfect. All the time I never took my eyes from her. As she returned around the end of the altar to her seat I followed her with my eyes. Not a word had been spoken—not even a whisper. She sat down. I continued to look at her until she raised her head. It was evident that she had been completely oblivious of others in the room. Her entire concentration was on her ravishingly beautiful daughter. Instead of a look of embarrassment on her face there was a radiance of righteous pride—not for the dress on which she had been working for months, which was beautiful beyond description, but for the daughter whom she had been molding with loving care for the previous twenty years. A mother's love could not have been more beautifully portrayed. I choked and said, "This is the most beautiful sight I have ever seen," which indeed it was.

We proceeded with the marriage and sealed the bride and groom as husband and wife for time and all eternity. The room was filled with the Holy Spirit and the guests sniffled and shed tears of joy. Indeed I had a glimpse of heaven that day.

$\mathscr{I}$ Would Be Worthy

Hugh B. Brown

I thank thee, Lord, that thou hast called me "son,"
And fired my soul with the astounding thought
That there is something of thee in me.
May the prophecy of this relationship—
    Impel me to be worthy.

I am grateful for a covenant birth;
For noble parents and an ancestry who beckon me
To heights beyond my grasp, but still attainable
If with stamina and effort I cultivate their seed—
    And prove that I am worthy.

I am grateful for a companion on this Eternal Quest,
Whose roots and birth and vision match my own;
Whose never-failing faith and loyalty have furnished light in darkness,
And re-steeled fortitude. May her faith in me
    Inspire me to be worthy.

I am grateful for the cleansing power of parenthood,
With its self-denial and sacrifice—prerequisites to filial and parent love;
For each child entrusted to our care, I humbly thank thee;
If I would associate with them eternally,
    I know I must be worthy.

I am grateful for the one who was recalled in youth,
For his love and loyalty and sacrifice.
May the memory of his clean and manly life keep resolute the hope
That I may renew companionship with him—and thee;
    For this I would be worthy.

I am grateful for the children of my children.
And, in anticipation, for others yet to be

Keep alive, I pray, within my bosom, a sense of obligation unto them,
To pass a name unsullied as it came. To become an honored sire,
    O make me worthy!

I am grateful for the lifting power of the gospel of thy Son;
For the knowledge thou hast given me of its beauty, truth and worth.
To attain its promised glory, may I to the end endure,
And then, forgiven, let charity tip the scales and allow me
    To be considered worthy.

"Why Haven't You Done My Temple Work?"

WENDY BRADFORD WRIGHT

When I was in the eighth grade, our English teacher, Mr. Duncan, introduced the class to the fascinating subject of family history. Through his assignment, I became acquainted with several of my ancestors, some of whom gave up much for religious freedom. My twelfth great-grandfather, William Bradford, became the governor of Plymouth colony after making the journey across the Atlantic on the *Mayflower*. At least two of his descendants became Methodist ministers, the same faith my parents chose to follow. Consequently I had been raised in a good churchgoing home, but we lacked the truths that bring full understanding.

During my teens, I had the opportunity to hear the gospel message, first from Latter-day Saint friends and then from the missionaries. During the missionary discussions, the concept that immediately caught my attention was that of eternal families. Was it really possible to again see my ancestors whom I'd grown to admire so much and my grandfathers who had died when I was young?

I began to soak up the gospel truths taught to me. I was baptized, and soon after I received my patriarchal blessing. I was told that I had come to earth through a noble lineage and that I should seek out my kindred dead. From these inspired words, I began to realize how important family history would become in my life. One of the phrases in my blessing stated, "You will be a Savior on Mount Zion for relatives who have gone on before you." I believed the words of the Prophet Joseph Smith: "The greatest responsibility in this world that God has laid upon us is to seek after our dead" (*Teachings of the Prophet Joseph Smith*, comp. Joseph Fielding Smith [Salt Lake City: Deseret Book Co.,

1977], p. 356). He also said that "those Saints who neglect it . . . do it at the peril of their own salvation" (ibid., p. 193).

Before I was married, I gathered the bits of information that my parents had obtained from other relatives. I planned to jump right into searching for ancestors further back on our pedigree, but as is so often the case my time got filled with other things, some important, some trivial. My ancestors were set on the shelf as I attended college and became engrossed in homemaking and impending motherhood.

Sometimes, though, our anxious ancestors are allowed to give us a swift kick to bring us back to the important matters of life. One night as I slept, I had a dream so real that to this day I can remember vivid details. My husband, Randal, and I were living in a small basement apartment in Provo, Utah, while we attended Brigham Young University. During the night, I suddenly awoke. I opened the bedroom door and, to my utter delight, found my Grandpa Bradford sitting on the old, ugly turquoise couch in our living room.

I had been thirteen when Grandpa died. We had been very close friends, and I admired and loved him greatly. His passing left a huge void in my life, one that seemed to get bigger instead of diminishing over time. Whenever I thought about Grandpa, I'd envision him floating in complete darkness with a sad look on his face. An intense fear of death enveloped me after his passing. I had never attended a funeral or seen a person who had passed away, and the thought of doing so brought a dread that was sometimes hard to shake. Even though my fears should have been squelched by the understanding I had gained from gospel principles, such as life after death and the resurrection, these fears were deeply imbedded and it was hard to fully grasp that these truths applied to me and my family.

Until I found my grandfather sitting on our couch! My previous fear of death was not present at all. It didn't seem strange to have Grandpa sitting there looking up at me. I wanted to run and throw my arms around him. I had missed him so much! But the look on his face made me stop quickly. It was apparent that he had been allowed to come for a specific reason. As I studied his face, I noticed that same sad look that had plagued my thoughts and dreams of the past.

Grandpa looked straight into my eyes and asked, "Why haven't you done my temple work?" I stood dumbfounded with a deep sense of guilt flowing over me, unable to reply. Again he asked: "Wendy, why haven't you done my temple work? Don't you realize that there are many, many people depending on you? You are the only person in the family who can help us!" The full impact of my responsibility as the only member of the Church in my family hit me, and I finally said, "I will, Grandpa, I will!"

The next morning I awoke feeling wonder about the event that had taken place the night before. I knew for a certainty that my grandfather had accepted the gospel truths in the spirit world, but he was unable to receive the needed ordinances there. A great desire welled up inside me to gather the necessary information so the saving ordinances could be performed for him and other relatives who were waiting. Joseph Fielding Smith said concerning the dead: "Thousands of men and women have died without knowing of Jesus Christ, or having an understanding of the nature of the laws of God; . . . All of these people are under the necessity of repentance and the Gospel will be taught to them in the world of spirits in its fulness. If they accept it there will be given to them the right of the essential ordinances administered vicariously in the Temples of the Lord, and they will become heirs in the celestial kingdom." (*Church History and Modern Revelation* [Melchizedek Priesthood study manual, 1949], pp. 136–37.)

When my husband and I walked into the baptistry at the Provo Temple a few weeks later, we immediately sensed an immense feeling of anticipation and joy. We knew that Grandpa was near and that the joy we felt was radiating from him and his sincere desire to be baptized. Randal was lowered into the waters of the baptismal font as Grandpa's proxy. We again experienced this happy feeling during the endowment session and later when Grandpa was sealed by proxy to his parents, along with his brothers and sisters.

From God's Point of View

Bonnie Ballif-Spanvill

Several years ago, my husband went into the hospital for a transfusion. While he was receiving the second unit of blood, he went into a coma. My father and my bishop came to the hospital to give him a blessing; they also blessed me, promising that the righteous desires of my heart would be granted unto me. I sat in the intensive care unit waiting for my husband to come out of the coma. I had lots of time to think. I prayed constantly. I talked to the Lord about Robert. I wanted so much for him to be well. Each time I began to pray, the words of the blessing I had received came strongly into my mind—the righteous desires of my heart would be granted. I wondered what could be more righteous than to have my husband live? My young children needed him! I was confident that my desire was righteous.

The long days passed. I continued to ponder and struggled to understand the righteous desires of my own heart. I finally realized that what I really wanted more than anything else was the greatest possible spiritual development for my husband, my three children, and for me. After that, if God could consider the cries of my heart and let my beloved live a little longer, that was what I wanted. I came to understand that the spiritual well-being of those I love was more important than his living or dying. A rush of the Spirit flowed through me and over me, assuring me that my righteous desires were also God's desires for me; we wanted the same thing. My thinking had been transformed. I went into that week wanting my husband to live at all costs, believing I had the faith for him to be healed. By the end of the week, I was humbled and grateful for the knowledge that whatever was needed to bring about the greatest spiritual well-being in my family was what I desired and God would do. I was beginning to learn how to see my personal struggles from God's point of view.

Missionary Work

*W*ith the Lord's Help

HUGH B. BROWN

Many years ago there was in many countries relentless and bitter opposition to the Church; the missionaries were frequently mobbed, whipped, driven out of cities, and sometimes martyred.

Then, as now, the missionaries learned to trust in and rely on the Lord for inspiration, protection, and guidance. The following missionary experience is related to illustrate how the Lord will come to the assistance of his servants if they do the best they can and have faith in him.

A young man, twenty-one years of age, arrived in England and was assigned by President Heber J. Grant to labor in the Norwich conference. His first assignment was to the city of Cambridge.

The last missionaries to labor in Cambridge before this young man arrived had been driven out of the city by an angry mob and were warned that if any Mormon elders came there again, they would do so at their peril.

This young man and his senior companion arrived in Cambridge on a certain Thursday afternoon in November 1904. They were immediately successful in obtaining a lodging place but were made uneasy and apprehensive as they saw across the road from their lodging large posters on the billboards, where they read among other things, "Beware of the vile deceivers; the Mormons are returning. Drive them out."

Friday morning the senior companion left for France as he was about ready to return home and had permission to take a trip on the continent. The young elder, therefore, was left alone. He had been instructed by his senior companion to go tracting that day, was told which streets to tract, and advised to tract at least five days a week.

He spent the rest of Friday morning and Friday afternoon tracting a certain street and on Saturday visited the university and other points of interest to get acquainted with the city.

Saturday evening as he sat in his lodging, a knock came at the door and he heard a man's voice inquire, "does an Elder _____ live here?" The young missionary, of course, thought the enemy had arrived, and he felt very lonely and somewhat afraid.

The landlady brought the man into the missionary's room, and he, producing a tract, asked, "Did you leave this at my door?"

The young man knew that his own name and address had been placed on the bottom of the tract by a rubber stamp and, though his fear almost prompted him to deny having delivered the tract, he knew that would be useless. He therefore said, "Yes, sir, I think I did leave that at your door if you live on _____ street."

The man then said to the young missionary, "Last Sunday a group of us left our church. We had a misunderstanding with the minister. We are not going back. We agreed among us that we would pray throughout the week that God would send us a new pastor. When I found this tract under my door as I came home this afternoon, I felt sure the Lord had answered our prayers. I communicated with my friends, and they agreed that I should come and see you. We wish you would come and be our pastor tomorrow night. I have a large home and a room big enough to accommodate my friends. There are seventeen of us in all, and we believe the Lord has sent you to us."

The young missionary was relieved to find the man was not an enemy, but in a sense he was more frightened at the prospects which lay ahead than he might have been if they had come to warn him to leave the city. He had not been in the mission field a week, had never attended a meeting in the mission field, had never presided in a meeting before going into the mission field, had never preached a sermon. To be now suddenly confronted with the prospect of holding a meeting without anyone to help him, without a companion, without preparation, took all the courage he could muster to say to the man, "Yes, sir, I will be pleased to come and be your minister tomorrow night." The man thanked him and left.

As the young man sat alone in his room after his visitor had gone, he was both excited and depressed. He knew that he had come three thousand miles for the express purpose of preaching the gospel and now an exceptional opportunity had presented itself, but he felt wholly inadequate, wholly unprepared, so completely dependent that he almost wished he had not promised to undertake the task.

When the landlady came in to prepare his evening meal, he told her he thought he would not eat that night. He went to his bedroom early. He knelt by his bed and talked with God. He did not say, "Now I lay me down to sleep." He told the Lord what his problem was and how he was there alone with no other Latter-day Saint within a hundred miles to his knowledge, that here were people seeking for the truth, and he pleaded with the Lord to come to his assistance.

Several times during the night he got out of bed and knelt again in prayer. He could not sleep as he tried to visualize himself standing before a strange group who looked to him as a trained minister and expected more of him than he could possibly deliver.

After spending the long night alternately tossing on his bed and kneeling in humble prayer, daylight came, and he notified the landlady that he would not have breakfast. He walked out through the park, by the university, past King's College, Christ's Church. He saw many happy people, young and old, seeming to be without worries or responsibilities. He felt that the weight of the world was upon his shoulders.

Upon returning to his room at noon he again gave instructions he would not eat. He took another long walk in the afternoon and, as he walked, continued to pray. So sure was he that he could not meet this situation that he actually prayed that God would send such a rainstorm that no one would come to the meeting. But that prayer was not answered.

Time came for the evening meal, but he was not hungry. The time set for the meeting was 7 o'clock, and the clock ticked on. Finally he put on his long Prince Albert coat, his high silk hat, took his Bible and his walking cane, and started for the address which the man had given him.

The young man had been a cowboy before his mission. He felt very awkward in the missionary clothes, and if "Home on the Range" had been written at that time he likely would have been humming it as he longed for the freedom of the western prairies.

Upon arrival at the address he knocked on the door rather timidly. Apparently the man had been watching for him out of the window because almost before he knocked, the door was opened. The man bowed courteously and said, "Come in, Parson," and ushered him into a large room where seventeen of the man's friends were sitting. They all arose in honor of their new minister. He was shown to a little table and chair, and the people all sat expectantly.

In all his worrying he had not really thought just what he would have to do. It had not occurred to him that no one there would know a Mormon hymn, that he could not call on any of them to offer the opening or the closing prayer. He had not realized how completely that meeting was to be up to him. In desperation he announced the first hymn as, "Oh, My Father" and was stricken with a sense of loneliness as he suddenly realized he would have to sing the song alone. This he tried to do, and the result was awful.

After singing two verses of the hymn he thought it was time to pray and was really afraid to stand before that congregation and offer prayer. He therefore suggested that they all turn around and kneel at their chairs while he knelt and prayed. This they did.

The opening words of that prayer were, "Our Father who art in heaven. These people who are kneeling here before thee have come to hear thy word. I came from Canada to England for the purpose of teaching thy word. Without thy help, oh, God, they will be disappointed, and I will be disgraced. Please, God, speak to them through me."

As the boy thus prayed, all fear left him. There came over him a sense of peace and a feeling that all would be well. They arose from their knees, and he thought it best to dispense with the second hymn and began to speak. Through the inspiration of the Lord he spoke forty-five minutes to that group, and many times they shed tears as he bore his testimony. At the close of the meeting they came, all of them, and each in turn said much the same thing, "Why have we not heard these things before? This is what we have been praying for. This, we know now, is the gospel. Thank God for sending you to us." His tears mingled freely with theirs as together they worshiped God and thanked him for his blessings.

Before many months every man, woman, and child who attended that meeting joined the Church. Many of them are living in America now, and hundreds of others have heard and embraced the gospel through them.

The young man who had come to that meeting with dragging feet and heavy heart returned to his lodging seemingly walking in the air and with a heart bursting with praises to God for His goodness. He knew that he had only been the instrument which God had used that night to sow seeds of the gospel. Surely God does hear the prayers of His servants.

"Who Has Need of the Physician?"

CARLOS E. ASAY

One weekend when I had no Church assignments, I decided to attend a sacrament service in a local ward. I took my seat in front on the stand and watched the people gather. A few of the people who came in I knew; most I did not.

Just moments before the meeting started, I saw two missionaries come in through a side door with a woman—a very worldly-looking woman. It was obvious that she was new to the group because she looked apprehensively from side to side and had to be guided to her seat. She was dressed in faded jeans and a tight sweater, and her face was heavily made up. Her dark and hardened countenance seemed to reflect a life of sin that was frightening to contemplate.

I couldn't help but wonder who would be successful in influencing the other—she the missionaries, or the missionaries her. Immediately following the service, I sought out one of the missionaries and spoke with him privately about the woman he and his companion had brought to church. My initial question was: "Elder, where did you meet that worldly woman?" My tone of voice was Pharisaic, inferring that he had brought to church someone who was unworthy of the privilege of worshiping with our group. The missionary bristled a little bit, stood his ground, and replied, "Elder Asay, who has need of the physician, the sick or the whole?" (See Matthew 9:9–13.)

Well, he had backed me into a corner. How could I question or refute what he and his good companion were attempting to do for someone who was spiritually sick and in desperate need of help from Christ, the Great Physician?

All I could say in return was: "Be careful! Make certain that she doesn't tempt or contaminate you."

Time passed, and I almost completely forgot the incident. But some months later I attended a fast and testimony meeting in the same chapel. The crowd was much the same as before; some I recognized, some I didn't. One woman entered alone, walked down the aisle, and seated herself near the front of the chapel. She sat quietly, meditated, and waited for the start of the meeting. She was dressed tastefully and her face reflected a special saintliness. In fact, she was beautiful. There was something familiar about her, but I couldn't be sure whether I had ever seen her before. No one in the congregation seemed to worship as intently as she did during the service. She seemed to sing and pray with all her heart.

It was a fast Sunday. The bishop bore his testimony and then invited others to bear theirs. The beautiful young woman was the first to respond. She stepped to the pulpit and began to speak. Among other things she tearfully told of how the missionaries had literally fished her out of the gutter, encouraged her to repent, and introduced her to members of the Church and to the fulness of the gospel. It was then that I realized she was the woman dressed in jeans that I had seen in church with the missionaries only a few weeks before. A miraculous transformation had taken place through the efforts of two dedicated missionaries who looked upon the woman not as she was but as she could become.

Salvation's Song

SHELDON L. ANDERSON

In hope, we see the Other Side,
When choirs of Saints for all the years
Will join to sing the holy praise
Of God and of His Son.

And then, divided, they will go
Through Spirit World as choruses
To touch bewildered hearts of those
Still searching for the truth.

If spirits preach, then spirits sing.
And music's power will not fail
To soften souls from barrenness
To ground prepared for seeds.

An Admonition from a Higher Source

ORSON F. WHITNEY

Editor's Note: At the age of twenty-one, Orson F. Whitney, who later became an Apostle, was called to preach the gospel in the eastern states and was ordained to the office of a Seventy. Prior to the call, he had been looking at pursuing a career in the theater. He entered the field of labor on November 6, 1876, having as his companion Elder Amos Milton Musser, a seasoned missionary who had preached the gospel in many parts of the world. After a time, Elder Whitney was faced with what he indicated was "a real temptation."

Prior to leaving home, I had done little writing and less speaking, neither hoping nor caring for success along either line. But now I was seized with a strong desire to write, especially to describe scenes beheld and incidents noted during my travels. Forthwith I began a correspondence with the Salt Lake Herald—first, however, writing to the editor, Byron Groo, and asking him if that paper would publish what I might send. He promptly replied, "thanking me in advance" and encouraging me to proceed. I used as a nom de plume my budget-box name, "Iago."

My communications to the Herald, the first one dated March 14, 1877, leaped at once into popular favor. This gratified me, of course, but I became so absorbed in the correspondence that it encroached upon hours that should have been given to religious study. Elder Musser chided me for it. "You ought to be studying the books of the Church," said he. "You were sent out to preach the Gospel, not to write for the newspapers." I knew he was right, but still kept on, fascinated by the discovery that I could wield a pen, and preferring that to any other pursuit except the drama, my ambition for which had been laid aside.

Then came a marvelous manifestation, an admonition from a higher Source, one impossible to ignore. It was a dream, or a vision in a dream, as I lay upon my bed in the little town of Columbia, Lancaster County, Pennsylvania. I seemed to be in the Garden of Gethsemane, a witness of the Savior's agony. I saw Him as plainly as ever I have seen anyone. Standing behind a tree in the foreground, I beheld Jesus, with Peter, James and John, as they came through a little wicket gate at my right. Leaving the three Apostles there, after telling them to kneel and pray, the Son of God passed over to the other side, where He also knelt and prayed. It was the same prayer with which all Bible readers are familiar: "Oh my Father, if it be possible, let this cup pass from me; nevertheless not as I will, but as thou wilt."

As He prayed the tears streamed down his face, which was toward me. I was so moved at the sight that I also wept, out of pure sympathy. My whole heart went out to him; I loved him with all my soul, and longed to be with him as I longed for nothing else.

Presently He arose and walked to where those Apostles were kneeling—fast asleep! He shook them gently, awoke them, and in a tone of tender reproach, untinctured by the least show of anger or impatience, asked them plaintively if they could not watch with him one hour. There He was, with the awful weight of the world's sin upon his shoulders, with the pangs of every man, woman and child shooting through his sensitive soul—and they could not watch with him one poor hour!

Returning to his place, He offered up the same prayer as before; then went back and again found them sleeping. Again He awoke them, readmonished them, and once more returned and prayed. Three times this occurred, until I was perfectly familiar with his appearance—face, form and movements. He was of noble stature and majestic mien—not at all the weak, effeminate being that some painters have portrayed; but the very God that He was and is, as meek and humble as a little child.

All at once the circumstance seemed to change, the scene remaining just the same. Instead of before, it was after the crucifixion, and the Savior, with the three Apostles, now stood together in a group at my left. They were about to depart and ascend into Heaven. I could endure it no longer. I ran from behind the tree, fell at His feet, clasped Him around the knees, and begged him to take me with Him.

I shall never forget the kind and gentle manner in which He stooped, raised me up, and embraced me. It was so vivid, so real. I felt the very warmth of His body, as He held me in His arms and said in tenderest tones: "No, my son; these have finished their work; they can go with me; but you must stay and finish yours." Still I clung to Him. Gazing up into His face—for He was taller than I—I besought Him fervently: "Well, promise me that I will come to you at the last." Smiling sweetly, He said: "That will depend entirely upon yourself." I awoke with a sob in my throat, and it was morning.

"That's from God," said Elder Musser, when I related to him what I had seen and heard. "I do not need to be told that," was my reply. I saw the moral clearly. I had never thought of being an Apostle, nor of holding any other office in the Church, and it did not occur to me even then. Yet I knew that those sleeping Apostles meant me. I was asleep at my post—as any man is who, having been divinely appointed to do one thing, does another.

But from that hour all was changed. I was never the same man again. I did not give up writing; for President Young, having noticed some of my contributions to the home papers, advised me to cultivate what he called my "gift for writing." "So that you can use it," said he, "for the establishment of truth and righteousness." I therefore continued to write, but not to the neglect of the Lord's Work. I held that first and foremost; all else was secondary.

"One Dirty Little Irish Kid"

HAROLD B. LEE

I remember the story that Brother Charles A. Callis used to tell us. There was a missionary who went over to Ireland and had filled a mission of two or three years. They invited him to the stand to give his homecoming speech and he said to them something like this, "Brothers and sisters, I think my mission has been a failure. I have labored all my days as a missionary here and I have only baptized one dirty little Irish kid. That is all I baptized."

Years later this man came back, went up to his home somewhere in Montana, and Brother Callis, now a member of the Council of the Twelve, learned where he was living, this old missionary, and he went up to visit him. And he said to him, "Do you remember having served as a missionary over in Ireland? And do you remember having said that you thought your mission was a failure because you had only baptized one dirty little Irish kid?"

He said, "Yes."

Well, Brother Callis put out his hand and he said, "I would like to shake hands with you. My name is Charles A. Callis, of the Council of the Twelve of The Church of Jesus Christ of Latter-day Saints. I am that dirty little Irish kid that you baptized on your mission."

They Couldn't Stop Reading

KEVIN STOKER

O n an April evening in 1988, ten young people began reading the Book of Mormon and didn't stop until they finished the next day. Most of them later investigated the Church, and some were baptized. The catalyst sparking this remarkable Book of Mormon conversion was an LDS girl whose love for an annual Easter pageant provided an opportunity for her nonmember friends to feel the Spirit.

As Lori Christlieb attended Green River College in Seattle, she became friends with several students who were in some of the same classes and ate lunch together every day. During the winter of 1988, Lori shared with them her strong feelings for the Easter pageant, "As I Have Loved You," sponsored by the Spokane Washington North Stake. Lori was from Spokane and played the trumpet in the orchestra for the pageant. She invited the students to attend, and ten of them accepted her invitation.

On Wednesday, April 6, 1988 these ten got into a van owned by a girl named Cathy and made the five-hour drive from Seattle to Spokane. After they watched the pageant, they stayed after to compliment Lori for her efforts. Lori struggled to hide her disappointment because she had wanted everything to be perfect for her friends but knew the performance hadn't been one of their best. However, a few days later, when she returned to Seattle and opened her mail, she realized that the quality of the music had not detracted from the outpouring of the Spirit.

The letter was from Cathy but represented the feelings of all of her friends who had attended the pageant. "We truly enjoyed it," Cathy wrote. Never in Cathy's life had she witnessed such a manifestation of the Savior's love. "We got in the van and started to head home," Cathy wrote. "There was silence and pondering of what we had just witnessed—except for Jake. He kept saying, 'Those people's spirits were so overwhelming.'"

Lori had given Sylvia, another member of the group, a Book of Mormon two days before leaving for Spokane. Sylvia hadn't read anything from the book, but she had brought it along on the trip to the pageant.

"After about an hour and a half on the road, and nonstop talking about the pageant, [we had] a feeling of calm come over us all," Cathy recalled. "Nita very quietly asked if she could see Sylvia's Book of Mormon."

Nita began reading aloud.

"It was as though we were all starving for the words it contained. I pulled the van to the side of the road, and there we started at the beginning. We could not let these words leave our minds, so we continued and did not stop until we reached the last verse, Moroni 10:34: 'And now I bid unto all, farewell. I soon go to rest in the paradise of God, until my spirit and body shall again reunite, and I am brought forth triumphant through the air, to meet you before the pleasing bar of the great Jehovah, the Eternal Judge of both quick and dead. Amen.'"

They had taken turns, each reading a chapter at a time. The time that passed had seemed short, but when they finished, they discovered their reading had taken them more than sixteen hours. It was 5:16 P.M. Thursday!

Cathy then recalled the night when Lori testified to the true meaning of the pageant as a way to worship the Savior. Lori also had told them about the spiritual leadership of the director and how she motivated the musicians to be in touch with the meaning of the music they were rehearsing, so this feeling could be conveyed to the audience. In this respect, Cathy wrote, the performers had been successful. "In no way did the mistakes take away from the reverence and get in the way of us witnessing such a glorious event!

"I probably speak for everyone [in saying] we never expected to be so fully and totally moved as we were that night."

As a postscript, Cathy noted that Lori probably would be happy to hear that Scott, Ted, Kate, Sylvia, Jake, Nita, and herself had scheduled to start taking the missionary lessons as a group in Nita's home April 16, 1988. "I for one am very anxious and excited to begin," Cathy concluded.

Lori moved back to Spokane soon after the pageant. Since that eventful night, she hasn't had any contact with these friends on whom she had such a profound influence. However, she learned from another student she had known at the college that four of the ten had been baptized. She could count those as the first of many she would introduce to the gospel, for she soon became Sister Lori Christlieb serving in the Peru Lima North Mission.

The World's Great Heart Is Aching

AUTHOR UNKNOWN

The world's great heart is aching,
    Aching fiercely in the night;
And God alone can heal it,
    And God alone give light;
And the ones to take that message—
    To bear the living word
Are you and I, my brothers
    And my sisters who have heard.

The Hairdresser

ROBERT E. WELLS

A pair of hardworking, constantly praying missionaries were trying to motivate a sister member to find a referral. She was a hairdresser and worked in a high-style shop in a nice area of the city. Her excuse for not giving any referrals in the past was that she didn't know anyone outside of the Church. She said she had been a member so long that all her friends were already members.

The missionaries insisted that if she were afraid to approach her nonmember neighbors and did not have any nonmember friends, she could ask the golden questions of her customers. She responded by saying that she did not dare offend any of her regular customers by talking to them about religion.

These forthright missionaries were not ready to give up. They wanted to commit the sister to become a finding member. The Elders reminded her that President David O. McKay had said, "Every member a missionary." They promised her that if she would pray for opportunities, the Lord would open the door. They made her an offer of a special miracle blessing if she would only try their idea.

The senior companion, being bold and led by the Spirit, with total faith said, "Sister, we promise you that if you will pray every morning for an opportunity to ask the golden questions, the Lord will send you a brand new customer whom you won't be afraid of offending. When the Lord does that, here is what you should do: When the new customer sits in your chair, you offer her the Book of Mormon to read. Will you do that?"

The hairdresser, looking for an excuse, responded, "I don't have a copy of the Book of Mormon to give away." The Elder was equal to that. "Here is a new copy for you to use. When your customer reads a little, then you ask the golden questions. Is that okay? Will you do that with a prayer in your heart for this miracle?"

153

The member sister wasn't sure if she could. Her excuse this time was, "And what if she recognizes that it is a religious book and wants a magazine to read instead?" The alert missionary responded easily, "Then here is a family home evening manual and a Church magazine, the *Liahona*. Both are brand new. If your new customer won't read the Book of Mormon, try the family home evening manual. If she won't read that, try the Church magazine. The Spirit will guide you. Then you can ask the golden questions. Do you remember what they are?"

The sister remembered very well what they were. The missionaries had repeated them so often she couldn't forget them. She nodded her head, smiled at how positive and confident they seemed, and accepted the reading material.

Later that day the miracle happened. A young woman had an unexpected social obligation and her usual hairdresser at another shop could not take her. She came in hurriedly and found that the only hairdresser with an empty chair was the Church member. The new customer explained her dilemma and the urgency and asked, "Can you take me right now even if I'm not a regular customer?"

The member sister was amazed that the missionary's promise seemed to be taking place. As soon as her patron was seated the member offered her the Book of Mormon to read. The customer opened it, noted the double columns, no illustrations, read only a few words, and remarked, "No thanks, this is too religious. What else do you have to read?"

The hairdresser then offered the family home evening manual. It should have been appreciated because the new customer's marriage and family situation was not only bad, it was on the verge of disaster. Unfortunately, the new lady turned to a chapter that again gave the impression of being very religious. She did not notice that it was especially for families just like hers and that it could have helped save them. Instead she closed it up, offered it back, and said to the hairdresser, "No thanks—just give me a magazine."

The hairdresser marveled that the Elder had anticipated all of this and had given her a new *Liahona* magazine. The new customer opened it near the middle, right at an article titled, "The Ideal Family," and began to read about families who pray together, who read the scriptures together, who go to church together, who speak loving words to each other, and where the father leads spiritually like the patriarchs of the Bible. After reading carefully the entire article the new customer remarked, "What a wonderful thing it would be to find a family like this one described here."

The member was so excited she blurted out, "How much do you know about my church?" The customer asked, "What is the name of your church?" She had not even noticed the name of the Book of Mormon. "The Church of Jesus Christ of Latter-day Saints, your friends the Mormons." "Oh yes," remarked the customer. "I have seen the missionaries on the street and have heard of the Mormon Tabernacle Choir in the United States on television. I have a friend who lives next to one of your chapels and says you sing nice hymns."

The member hairdresser had been praying for just such an opportunity. "Would you like to know how our church got started and how we can have ideal families like the family in the article you were reading? Our missionaries can tell you better than I can. You can come to my home, even though it is very humble . . . or I can bring them to your home."

The young woman preferred to set up an appointment at her home during siesta time a couple of days later. The hairdresser and the missionaries went to a very nice home in an exclusive part of the city. The lady listened to the missionaries with interest and attention. She even offered the prayer at the end of the first visit.

That evening this young mother announced to her husband that she had invited some Mormon missionaries and a Mormon hairdresser to her home—and she liked what they were teaching! The husband didn't appear to understand or even listen to what she was saying. She repeated what she had said and announced, "I think we ought to listen to the missionaries as a family—you, me, and the children. It would do us some good. They can tell us how to have an ideal family." The husband understood just enough to mumble, "It's okay for you and the kids but not for me." Bravely, she interrupted his reading and insisted, "We are *all* going to listen to these Mormon missionaries, or I am going to take the children home to Chicago!"

Their marriage was on the verge of divorce. They were living in a Latin American country. She was Spanish speaking, but her family lived in Chicago. He loved his kids and didn't want to lose them. He gave in. "Okay, we'll listen to them, but we won't join their church."

After a few visits by the missionaries, the husband liked what he was hearing. He wanted to please his wife and keep her and the kids with him in Latin America, but he was still determined to not join the Church.

After the discussions with the family, the original baptismal date the missionaries had mentioned in the first discussion was fast approaching. She asked her husband what he was going to do. He said, "You and the kids can get baptized. I am not ready yet. I still smoke, I still drink occasionally, and I cannot see paying tithing on the money we make." She was even more direct and forceful this time. "If you don't get baptized with us, I am taking the kids home to Chicago." He knew her threat was real. She had her own influential relatives, and she had her own funds. She could do what she wanted to do, and he probably could not stop her.

He smilingly told me later that he was baptized under duress, coercion, force, and threats from his wife. He said that he felt the gospel was true but that he was not ready to change. But he agreed to be baptized to please his wife.

The Elder who was voice in the confirmation made an unusual promise. He blessed the husband that his body would not be able to tolerate any substance contrary to the Word of Wisdom and that he would be greatly blessed if he were faithful to the law of tithing.

My wife and I were with them in the temple one year from their date of baptism as they were sealed to each other and to their children. He told me of his being tempted with tobacco and alcohol, but they caused him great nausea to the point that he lost all interest. And when he forgot his tithing, he was immediately reminded with a drop in profits, but when he was faithful, everything went right in his businesses.

The family became great assets to the Church. This story is one of my favorites to illustrate how a member can become a finding missionary using the golden questions, prayer, and faithful, sweet boldness.

If we really want to be part of hastening the Lord's missionary work, we will pray every day for opportunities, ask the golden questions to find out if people are among the elect today, and if they are, we will invite them to our home "day after tomorrow, after dinner" to hear the missionaries explain the origin of The Church of Jesus Christ of Latter-day Saints. Be sweetly bold, positive, and happy, and you will win friends, bless people's lives, and increase baptisms.

Coming Home

GEORGE D. DURRANT

The English have an old saying which states, "Go to sea, son, if for no other reason than the glory of coming home."

Multiply a seaman's homecoming by a thousandfold and you'll catch at least a dim vision of the glory of a returning missionary.

When my son returned home from his mission, we were all at the airport an hour in advance of the scheduled arrival of his plane. As I waited, I found myself unable to carry on a sensible conversation. I had never been so nervous. I call it nervousness, but I'm not sure that is what it was. It was an undescribable inner emotional sensation that only comes a few times in an entire lifetime. And the closer the time of his arrival came, the more the wonderful sensation intensified within my soul.

I found myself wondering: "What will I do? What will I say? How will I act?"

On schedule the plane touched down. Through the glass windows I watched the doorway of the huge jet come open. People began to pour out. My son was not the first to disembark, nor was he among the first ten. I panicked a little as I wondered, "Did he miss the plane?"

I pressed my nose against the glass pane and counted—out came twenty more passengers. He was still not among them. I almost shouted at my wife: "Are we in the correct place? Is this the right flight?"

Fifty more exited—then a hundred more and a thousand (at least it seemed that many). Then came a break in the flow of deplaners and no more came. All of us who awaited were speechless. My so-called excitement had now become concern.

A second or two later the pilot came out. Then the ramp was empty again. But wait, another surge of hope. Two more passengers appeared and came down the stairs.

And then after another second or two, when I was sure he would not come, he appeared. With bags in hand and looking down to be sure of his step, he walked down the stairs to the ground and then he began to walk the thirty or so yards to the terminal. I watched his every step. I was spellbound at seeing him.

He came through the door. His seven brothers and sisters surrounded him. A broad smile crossed his face. His mother greeted him warmly.

And from my rearward position I came ever closer. Somehow the other family members stood aside and soon I stood face to face with my son. I looked into his eyes. And without any outward reasoning I embraced him and held him close to me, and I cried.

I had wondered what I'd do and now I knew. The only way to properly express all of my feelings was to throw aside all words and just hold him close and cry with joy. We had walked nearly to the baggage claim before I could speak any coherent sentences.

I've never been involved in anything so thrilling as the return of my missionary son.

And so, as a spokesman for all fathers and all mothers, I say to you, "Go on a mission, son, for a million reasons, among which is the glory of coming home."

$\mathcal{H}$e Picked "Mormons"

KEVIN STOKER

When Cadet Joe Tiemann selected a topic for a comparative religion class report, he looked down the long list of religious denominations and stopped at The Church of Jesus Christ of Latter-day Saints. "I don't know why I picked Mormons," Joe says. "I can't really give you a good reason. I can say I knew some LDS cadets [at the Air Force Academy]. One of them I knew pretty well, and I thought a lot of him. After I took on this particular project, I asked him several questions about Mormons."

It was 1970. Joe was a junior at the U.S. Air Force Academy in Colorado Springs, Colorado. In three years at the academy, his feelings about religion had changed dramatically. As a youth in Karnes City, Texas, he had attended the Southern Baptist Church with his family. But since coming to the academy, he had joined a nondenominational evangelical organization known as the Navigators. At that time, he felt membership in a particular denomination was not as important as one's relationship with God. So why was he researching the Mormons? Curiosity. Joe found the study of different religions fascinating.

Books on Mormons were plentiful. Most were objective, but some were critical and negative. Although he tried to maintain objectivity when he presented his report, Joe found himself agreeing more with the perception propagated by the anti-Mormon books.

In 1971 he graduated, then spent two months touring the western United States with a friend before reporting to McClellan Air Force Base in Sacramento, California. They stopped off in Salt Lake City and toured Temple Square. Their tour guide happened to be president of a local bank. "He was a very intelligent and articulate man who said a lot of things that, at first, I did not understand," Joe says. "But when he gave scriptural references for those doctrines, I would check them out, and he would be accurate. I couldn't understand why I had never seen [those scriptures] before."

After the tour, Joe and his friend wandered around the visitors' center and met a tour guide who was a retired army colonel. The young second lieutenants were awed by this former "full colonel." He left an indelible impression on the young men. For the next few days, Joe and his friend read through each of the pamphlets and discussed the Church's doctrines and beliefs. "After two or three days, we decided the Mormons were still incorrect," Joe says. "I kind of put the issue to rest, but something continued to gnaw at me, especially when I came across one of those Bible verses quoted by our tour guide."

At McClellan, he began attending a large fundamentalist church, and soon became one of the leaders of its 125-member youth group—even though he hadn't joined that denomination. He had fun but received little spiritual satisfaction. Once during a religious retreat, Joe met a prominent anti-Mormon minister, who was the guest speaker. "He came for a week and talked about every cult. I really was disturbed by and had objections to his attitude toward Mormons. It wasn't that I disagreed with his scriptural dissertation, but I really disagreed with his attitude because I thought it was not Christian."

At Joe's next duty assignment in Alaska, his insatiable desire to understand what other people believed led him to study the Eastern Orthodox faith. Meanwhile he also met Dale Goetz, a second lieutenant and returned missionary. Goetz's positive influence succeeded in keeping Joe interested in Mormonism.

From Alaska, Joe was transferred to Germany, where he continued to immerse himself in the Eastern Orthodox religion. He also studied Catholicism. But then he met two Mormon elders. "I was driving home from work in this blowing, driving snowstorm, and I saw two missionaries walking at what seemed to be a forty-five-degree angle against the wind," Joe relates. "I thought, 'I know who these guys are.'"

He picked the elders up and gave them a ride to his apartment. "I know why you're here, and I understand what you believe," he told the missionaries. "If you're ever over in my neighborhood, drop by." A couple of days later, the missionaries visited him, and others continued to drop by for more than a year. They gave him copies of the Book of Mormon, *Jesus the Christ, The Articles of Faith, A Marvelous Work and a Wonder,* and *The Restored Church.* From reading those books and talking with the missionaries, he developed a list of objections. However, when he returned to reading the Bible, he began seeing things in a different light and understanding scriptures in a way he had never done before. "I would see things in passages of scripture that I had memorized, and it was like seeing it from a totally new perspective."

A new set of missionaries would often ask him if he had prayed about the Church. "I felt like smacking them," he says. Of course, he had prayed. For him, accepting the Church wasn't a matter of getting a yes or no answer to prayer. He could believe some of the doctrines, but he refused to surrender on the big issue—the nature of God. To abandon his belief in the Trinity struck him as the ultimate heresy.

He left Germany with a desire to continue investigating the Church. Some of his Protestant friends found this interest in Mormons disturbing. He moved to San Antonio, Texas, and Randolph Air Force Base. Two months after buying a house, he was tracted out by two missionaries. "What took you so long?" he said. The missionaries began visiting regularly, often bringing stake missionaries, the local elders quorum president, and the bishop. Joe kept up his personal study by going to the local library and picking up eight to ten books on Mormonism, including *Gospel Ideals* by David O. McKay.

"Each day I read one chapter [of *Gospel Ideals*] at lunchtime, and, each time, I would come away thinking, 'What he is saying is true. If people live like this, they will be following Christ.'"

He continued studying for four or five months. One of those working with him was Sergeant Jim Edwards, a seventy whom Joe liked. Finally, Jim challenged Joe to be baptized. "You understand as much about the Church as I do," Jim said.

"I was waiting for him to say pray about it, so I could smack him, but he didn't. He said, 'Have you fasted about it?' and I said I hadn't."

Jim said he would fast until Joe found out whether the Church was true or not. It only took one day. Joe read through the New Testament and gained many new insights. He then prayed to gain a conviction that the Church was true. First, he accepted the general idea of prophets being called of God to direct His kingdom here on earth. From Joe's reading of the Book of Mormon, he knew Joseph Smith was a prophet. His existing testimony of David O. McKay's calling helped him realize that the Church continues to be led by a prophet. "Those three principles established a foundation," Joe recalls. "I called up Jim Edwards to tell him that I had made a decision to be baptized on Sunday."

On October 12, 1980, ten years after he began his study of Mormonism, Joe was baptized.

Gospel Lessons

The Former District President

ROBERT E. WELLS

I had the unique privilege of accompanying Elder Delbert L. Stapley, a great Apostle, when he was preparing to organize a stake out of a mission district in Mexico. This involved calling a stake presidency, twelve members of the high council, and bishoprics for the branches being changed to wards. The Apostle's requirements for all candidates who would be ordained to the Melchizedek Priesthood office of high priest were simple: experience as a Church leader and worthiness for a temple recommend. After many hours of interviews, some shuffling of people from one position to another, and even calling brethren back for a second or third interview, all positions were filled except for a twelfth high councilor. There was no one left who was both experienced as a Church leader and worthy enough to hold a temple recommend who could meet the established conditions for this last position.

The position of high councilor is certainly not the last normally filled. The high council serves together with the stake presidency in much the same kind of relationship that the Twelve Apostles serve with the prophet and the First Presidency. The calling of a high councilor is a very important and vital one, requiring strong and experienced leaders capable of supervising the wards and branches and auxiliary organizations, as well as attending to a number of other significant duties.

During the process of working to fill the high council, Elder Stapley decided to move some of the branch presidents to serve on the high council, and some of the local leaders who had previously been assigned to the district high council were called as bishops. When all this work was finished, we found that we had inadvertently not filled the position of the twelfth high councilor.

When we noted the remaining vacancy, we reviewed the list of men who had not been called but found no one who was both worthy enough and experienced enough, according to the Apostle's desires. Finally, in some frustration, Elder Stapley interrupted, saying, "Well then, please go find me a former district president who is inactive. We'll put *him* on the high council!" That seemed to be somewhat of a contradictory request. Again, we reviewed the list of men we had interviewed, including some less active than others that had not been invited to be interviewed, and we couldn't find anyone who fit this great Apostle's expectations. I relayed that message to Elder Stapley, whose response was even more startling. "Oh, you've always got an inactive district president around. Go find him." I honestly didn't think we had overlooked anyone, but he was insistent and sent me out to inquire from some of the pioneer members who were still waiting for interviews or were involved in the preparation of the special conference.

I inquired of a long-time member, an older man, who was waiting to be interviewed for another position in the new stake. He responded by saying, "Yes, there is one whom you have not interviewed, but I don't think you can use him—he is totally inactive. He hasn't attended any meetings for a long time, he has a Word of Wisdom problem I think, and doesn't pay any tithing. Some years ago he was offended by a gringo mission president and he went inactive. He is mad at all the gringos in the Church."

I went back to Elder Stapley with the disappointing news. I repeated the information verbatim. His reaction was a revelation to me and something I have always remembered. "Maybe *you* don't want to call him to the high council, maybe *I* don't want to call him to the high council, but I have a feeling that the *Lord* wants him called. Please send someone to bring him in for an interview. If he doesn't want to come, tell him that an Apostle of the Lord is asking him to come." This was surprising to me, both because this contradicted the Apostle's initial instructions and because it seemed to come as a revelation of the Lord's will at that very moment to an Apostle who seemed to be as astonished as I was.

We followed his instructions to send a car with two members who knew this former district president well. They brought him back, but he was obviously displeased. Nevertheless, our reluctant guest had taken the time to dress in a white shirt, tie, and suit. That impressed me greatly. I was afraid that he might come in a sporty *guayabera* (an open-necked shirt) to broadcast his disapproval. He was an unusually handsome man with a full head of wavy hair—very much like the actor Cesar Romero—with a nicely trimmed mustache.

When he appeared at the office door, Elder Stapley took him by the hand and never let go. He led him into the room, indicating to me to close the door. The Apostle sat down on a couch, pulling this brother down beside him. There they sat, hand in hand, knee touching knee, and looking at each other eye to eye. I sat to one side translating, although it seemed they did not need me.

Elder Stapley was very candid, as was his style. "Do you love your Heavenly Father?" was his first question. Direct and succinct. The former district president's response was just as direct and abrupt. "Sí!" he blurted out loudly and firmly with a scowl of displeasure as if to say, it seemed to me, "Yes! I'm just as close to God as any of you gringos."

Elder Stapley did not flinch nor lower his gaze. He continued, "Do you love your Savior, Jesus Christ?" "Sí . . ." The man's voice was softer, as if to say, "Yes, but where is this going?" because his voice started low and then rose in a questioning tone. I was immediately aware that something unusual was happening. Our man's resistance seemed to be dissipating in the presence of an Apostle.

Elder Stapley then asked a third question. "Do you love the Church of Jesus Christ, your Savior? *This* church?" The man hung his head, began to weep, and answered contritely and softly, "Sí. Amo a la Iglesia." ("Yes, I do love the Church.")

His tears were flowing with visible emotion. The Apostle did not hesitate. He declared firmly, "Then I am calling you to be ordained a high priest and to take your place in the high council of this new stake of Zion." The man's head was still bowed, his eyes seemed closed. He responded, shaking his head, "I'm sorry, I can't accept. I am inactive."

Elder Stapley, still holding his hand, insisted, "I did not ask that. Will you accept the call?" The good brother looked up then, and through his tears explained, "You don't understand. I really am inactive. I am not attending church. I haven't observed the Word of Wisdom. I am not paying my tithing. I was offended by—" Cutting him off in midsentence, Elder Stapley interrupted sternly but lovingly and with authority, "I did not ask that either." And with added emphasis, he repeated: *"Will you accept the call?"*

I could not tell, but I am sure that Elder Stapley must have squeezed his hand as if to reassure him of his love or perhaps to encourage him, because the good brother acted startled, hesitated, then cautiously said, "Well, I'll do anything you tell me to do." I sensed that the intent and implication was as if to say, "You really wouldn't dare call me, an inactive man, to such a high calling, would you? I'll call your bluff by saying I'll do what you tell me to do."

The inspired Apostle responded positively, "You will do *anything* I tell you to do? Fine. Then you will accept the call! Will you accept the call?" The fellow nodded in surprise. It wasn't turning out like he thought it would. Elder Stapley continued, "And will you attend all your meetings from now on?" The good brother nodded and answered, "Sí." It was beginning to dawn on him that he had made a promise to an Apostle to do anything the Apostle told him to do and the Apostle was taking him up on it.

"And will you observe the Word of Wisdom totally and completely from now on?" Elder Stapley asked. "Yes," he answered. "It isn't a big problem—it won't be any problem at all." It was obvious that the former Church leader was gathering more spiritual strength and self-confidence as the interview continued.

"And will you pay a full tithing from now on?" queried Elder Stapley. With increasing assurance, and now with a strong voice, the brother replied, "Yes, I will. I was always greatly blessed when I was paying a full tithing. I'll do it again." Elder Stapley wasn't through. "Do you love your wife, and are you faithful to her?" The reply was convincing: "Yes, and I have always been faithful to her."

Then came a question I had never expected, but which, in view of the circumstances, was surely appropriate. Elder Stapley looked him in the eye and slowly and deliberately, with emphasis, asked, "And will you forgive all the gringos in the Church?" For a moment I thought we had lost him. He looked down at the floor. He moved his head slowly from side to side, not shaking it in a disapproving way but rather showing inner turmoil as he worked things out in his head and his heart. Then maybe Elder Stapley squeezed his hand again, because suddenly, and unexpectedly, this repentant former district leader looked up into Elder Stapley's eyes. All he saw was love—an Apostle's love, a Christlike love, a love that could change a person's heart. A powerful spiritual electricity ran between those two hands and those two sets of eyes. He saw or felt no criticism, no judging—just love—and love won.

The wavy-haired, handsome former district president said softly and humbly, "Yes, I'll forgive everybody. I guess it's about time." Elder Stapley stood and embraced him with a big Latin hug of male fellowship and confidence, welcoming a lost coin back into the kingdom. I had seen a miracle of reactivation take place.

Sunday morning, when I presented the names for the sustaining vote, I went through the new stake presidency easily. There were no opposing votes. Then I went through the list of new high councilors. When I reached the name of the former leader, I pronounced it very clearly, and as I had expected, there was a stir in the audience. I looked up and saw a few turn to their companions and whisper, "Could it be?" And, with a shake of their heads, the response was, "No, it couldn't be him. He's inactive!" Each man named had been asked to stand as his name was called out. I waited for this special man to stand. People turned to look. They saw that grand old leader who had done so much to build the Church back when the Church was new. In fact, he was the leader who had organized the members to do their part in the construction of the large chapel in which we were meeting, in the days when the members committed to dig the foundations, pour the concrete, do the concrete block work, and the rest of the labor that was their share of the construction cost. Those members who knew him, loved him and appreciated his past service and sacrifices. When I called for the vote, some raised *both* hands in support. All of us were crying tears of joy. We had witnessed a miracle.

As I look back on this unforgettable incident, I am impressed that Elder Stapley did not hesitate to run a risk by calling a lost coin (who might just as well have been a lost sheep or a lost prodigal) to an important position. Neither did he suggest to us that we wait for a period of time to make sure that a change of heart had really taken place. I observed that Elder Stapley did not remind the good brother that he who is offended has the greater sin than the one who did the offending. Elder Stapley didn't do anything other than love that great man, offer him a responsible position in the Church, recognize his talents and abilities, and call him to serve again. Elder Stapley's courage and inspiration were amply rewarded. That good brother kept his promise and remained active from that time forth.

"Why Don't You *Really* Pray About It?"

H. Burke Peterson

I suppose we have all had someone do something to us that we didn't like, and that made us angry. We can't forget it, and we don't want to be around that person. This is called being unforgiving. Now, the Lord has had some very strong words to say to those who will not forgive one another. Many years ago I had an experience with being unforgiving. I felt I had been taken advantage of, and I did not like the person. I did not want to be around him; I would pass on the other side of the street if he came down it; I wouldn't talk to him. Long after the issue should have been closed, it was still cankering my soul. One day my wife, who is very astute and knows when I'm not doing everything I should, said, "You don't like so and so, do you?"

"No, I don't," I said. "But how could you tell?"

"Well, your feelings show—in your countenance it shows. Why don't you do something about it?" she asked.

"Like what?"

"Why don't you pray about it?"

I said, "Well, I did pray once, and I still don't like him."

"No," she replied, "Why don't you *really* pray about it?"

Then I began to think, and I knew what she meant. So I decided that I was going to pray for a better feeling about this person until I had one. That night I got on my knees, and I prayed and opened up my heart to the Lord. But when I got up off my knees, I still didn't like that person. The next morning I knelt and prayed and asked to have a feeling of goodness toward him; but when I finished my prayers, I still didn't like him. The next night I still didn't like him; a week later I didn't like him; a month later I didn't like him—and I had been praying every night and every morning.

I kept it up, and finally I started pleading—not just praying, but pleading. After much prayer, the time came when without question or reservation I knew I could stand before the Lord, if I were asked to, and that he would know that at least in this instance my heart was pure. A change had come over me after a period of time. That stone of unforgiveness needs to be removed from all of us, if it happens to be there; and I suggest that persistent prayer might be a way to remove it.

Where Home Is

ANNE OSBORN POELMAN

The General Authorities' traditional July break is a much needed time for rest and recuperation. No stake or regional conferences are scheduled during the month and the relentless meeting schedule temporarily subsides.

Ron, my husband, and I usually take the opportunity to escape Salt Lake City's summer heat for a few days. Several years ago we decided to visit Santa Fe, New Mexico. I had seen an appealing ad in *Sunset* magazine that touted the pleasant days, cool evenings, and multicultural charm of the old territorial capital. We tried it, liked it, and have been going there ever since.

Our favorite spot is the Bishop's Lodge, a quiet, rustic place nestled in Tesque Canyon at the foot of the Sangre de Cristo mountains. The Bishop's Lodge is famed as the site of Willa Cather's *Death Comes for the Archbishop*.

There's no longer a bishop at the Bishop's Lodge. But they do have horses. Lots of them. I grew up with horses and love to ride. The first time we stayed at the Lodge, I noticed an attractively illustrated poster near the registration desk advertising "Breakfast Rides."

"Ron, look! They have horses!"

He grimaced.

I ignored his dubious look. "See, it says here, 'For riders of all experience levels, novice to expert.'"

"I've never reached a satisfactory accommodation with a horse," he said.

Hoping to convince him by appealing to his stomach, I rambled on. "It also says, 'Genuine Western chuck-wagon breakfast.'"

Ron's a good sport. "Well, I'm willing to give it a try," he conceded gracefully.

We signed up. As requested, we listed age, weight, and riding experience. I put down "experienced." Peeking over Ron's shoulder, I watched him write, "Never been on a horse before."

I protested. "That's not true. You told me you've been riding once or twice before!"

"Only after a fashion," he replied. "When I was nine or ten years old, we visited some relatives who lived on a farm in southern Utah. While the adults were talking, I went exploring. I saw a horse standing inside the corral with a saddle on its back. So I sneaked up, walking along the fence utnil I was just above it. Then I jumped into the saddle. The next thing I remember was waking up, lying in bed with a beefsteak on my eyes!"

I was horrified.

"You can guess what had happened," he continued. "The horse was a two-year-old colt they were just starting to break. My uncle had put the saddle on the horse's back so he'd get used to it before someone actually rode him for the first time. He'd never been ridden before. So when I innocently jumped into the saddle he bucked me off in a split second, and I hit my head on the ground. I was out cold."

I shuddered, "And have you ever been riding since?"

"Nope," he concluded with finality.

Now I understood his reluctance, his claim of complete inexperience, and what a good sport he was to try again.

The next morning we rose bright and early, reporting to the head wrangler, Carol Thorpe. She called the numerous guests one by one, assigning each to a horse her practiced eye told her would be an appropriate match. "Anne?" she said, checking her clipboard.

"Here!" I replied promptly.

"Experienced rider?"

"Yes," I said, with more confidence than I felt.

"You're on Buck," she said, pointing out a handsome buckskin gelding. "Ron?"

He stepped forward smartly. "Here!"

"You listed, 'Never been on a horse before'?"

"Well, only once, and that was very briefly. It wasn't a satisfying experience—for me *or* the horse!" he answered with a wry smile.

"Well, then," she chuckled, "we'll put you on Nehi. He's a horse we use for beginners and children."

Ron looked relieved. While the other guests were saddling up and having stirrups adjusted, he was reading something intently. I didn't know what it was at the time, but later discovered it was a reprint of an article that Carol's husband, Jim, had written for the local newspaper. It was titled "How to Ride a Horse."

One by one, the various groups of riders started out on the Lodge's extensive trail system. For over an hour we meandered through the stands of sweet-smelling piñon pines and junipers that covered the red rock foothills below the Santa Fe National Forest. Clumps of fragrant sagebrush, chamisa, and scrub oak accented the spectacular scenery. Black-chinned and broad-tailed hummingbirds whirred overhead in the startlingly blue sky. Small, squirrel-like animals chattered and scolded as we rode by their burrows.

We finally emerged onto a broad, flat mesa where we were met by the tantalizing smells of sizzling bacon, griddle cakes, and jalapeño seasoned fried potatoes with onions. That kind of stuff just about goes straight from your mouth to your coronary arteries without even passing through your stomach!

It tasted wonderful.

"Well, what do you think?" I asked Ron between mouthfuls.

"About the food or the ride?"

"Both."

"Great!" he replied with a broad grin. "I really enjoyed the food *and* the ride."

"How 'bout going again tomorrow?" I asked eagerly.

"Whoa! Let's see how we feel when we get up in the morning. I might be a little sore," he demurred.

He felt fine the next day so we went again, this time on a little longer ride. Despite his unfortunate early childhood experience, Ron had a natural riding ability that amazed both himself and the wranglers. He soon graduated to a more lively horse and was finally "promoted" to Chief Joseph, a tall, gangly Appaloosa that quickly became his favorite mount. As Ron's confidence grew, we gradually extended the rides onto steeper, more challenging trails.

He loved it.

Every night after dinner we trekked out to the corral like a couple of kids, pockets stuffed with carrots and apples for the horses. Buck soon recognized our footsteps and headed toward the fence when he heard us coming, laying his ears back and warning the other horses off with a dismissive snort. Joe, shy and unaggressive, usually hung back until Ron coaxed him up with soft clucks and gentle words of encouragement.

When we returned to Salt Lake City, Ron eagerly recounted his horseback riding adventures to his brothers. He attributed much of his initial success to reading Jim Thorpe's helpful hints. "I never realized you're supposed to ride using you legs, not your seat!" he enthused.

Keith, the youngest, laughed. "Well, sure, Ron. You can learn to do a lot of things if you can read!"

The following January, Ron was sorting though the mail one evening as I fixed dinner. His face brightened. "Ha! We just got our reservations confirmed for next summer at the Bishop's Lodge," he announced.

"You're excited," I responded.

"I miss Joe," he confessed somewhat sheepishly. "I'm really looking forward to seeing him again."

"I'm not jealous," I teased. "It's okay to have an additional 'significant other'—as long as it's a horse!"

The next summer, Ron was eager to return to Santa Fe and could hardly wait for our first ride. When we approached the corral, Joe whickered at Ron in recognition. Ron, inordinately pleased, exclaimed, "He remembers me!"

Indeed he did.

As we saddled up and headed into the mountains, Ron and Joe hung back a bit. Joe was walking placidly, one ear flopped over in relaxation and eyes half closed in pleasure as Ron mur-

mured to him quietly. Every line of Ron's body bespoke pure enjoyment.

Denusha, one of our favorite wranglers, looked back and chortled. "I don't know who's more contented," she commented, "the man or the horse!"

Near the end of our stay, Ron and I were both eager to venture beyond the well-worn Lodge trails. Denusha offered to take us on a long private ride to the aspen meadows high in the Sangre de Cristo mountains.

We packed lunches, water, and the sketchy hiking maps we had found in local mountainneering stores. A brief rainstorm during the night had freshened the sparkling air and dampened the dirt trails. The pines and junipers emitted pungent odors as we brushed by them on our way up the mountain.

Ron rode Joe, of course. I was on Buck, the handsome gelding; he was well into the equine equivalent of middle age but still loved to gallop until the wind made my eyes tear. Denusha was on Mercedes, a spirited, coal-black mare of indeterminate lineage and disproportionate conformation who nevertheless had the stamina of a well-conditioned triathlete.

The horses, eager and well rested, walked so fast we were at the aspen meadow before lunchtime. Denusha looked at her watch and grinned mischievously. "We've still got lots of time left," she announced. "Want to go exploring?"

"Sure!" we both exclaimed enthusiastically.

She gave Mercedes a squeeze with her legs and off they went, straight up the side of a steep hill, propelled like a rocket by the mare's powerful hindquarters.

We followed. Before long we were riding on unkempt, rarely used trails. Overhanging branches and dense undergrowth lined the narrow paths, scraping against us as the horses wove back and forth between the closely spaced trees.

We retraced our route several times, following the barely visible trail. Eventually the faint track petered out completely, ending blindly on a steep ridge that overlooked a box canyon.

Denusha paused, then pulled out the map. A bad sign.

"We're not lost, are we?" I asked anxiously.

"Naw," Ron put in with good humor. "We're not lost. We just don't know where we are!"

I didn't think that was very funny. When I didn't laugh, his smile faded. "Are we really lost, Denusha?" he questioned soberly.

"Yep," she replied. Strangely enough, she didn't seem worried. Not in the least.

"Why aren't you worried?" I demanded, somewhat annoyed at her casual attitude.

"'Cause the horses aren't lost," she answered calmly. "*We* may be lost. But *they* always know which way home is. Especially good ol' Buck. He knows for sure."

I was astonished. "You mean all those old stories about lost or injured cowboys tying themselves into the saddle during a blizzard and the horse taking them all the way home are for real?"

"Sure," she replied matter-of-factly. "Watch. You lead. Just let Buck have his head."

"Okay," I said dubiously, nudging Buck to the front of our threesome. I would have bet he had never been on that overgrown trail so far from the Lodge's familiar territory.

Buck strode out confidently and steadily. Neck arched proudly, his ears swiveled forward in watchful alertness as he led our small group down the mountain.

You can guess the end of the story. Three hours and a brief lunch break later, we were back at the corral. Faithful Buck was rewarded with an extra ration of bran mash. We took a hot bath.

One of the most comforting, reassuring things I've learned as a convert to the Church is that the Brethren always know where "home" is. *Always*. Outsiders may think it naïve and doubters may scoff, but I firmly believe you simply can't go wrong by following the First Presidency and the Twelve. They know the sure way, even when the trail seems faint or imperceptible to the rest of us.

A Lesson from My Son

RAND PACKER

One time we older boys had inadvertently left a tube of toxic model airplane glue on the table where we had been working. Our little one-year-old Tiffany reached up on the table and found it to be a gooey treat. We discovered her gleefully gulping it down. The next few minutes were clouded with tears and emergency calls and worthless excuses, but they were also brightened with a godly tribute to youth. As mom, dad, and family scurried around the home with advice and orders, there was one among us who was greater. I barged into the bathroom to get a washcloth and was surprised to discover my young son Trevor kneeling before Heavenly Father and pleading for the life of his little sister. He was embarrassed as he stood quickly, and he didn't know what to say. But he didn't need to say anything, because his actions spoke and I knew what he was doing. In that moment of minor crisis it was a young boy who turned to God while the oldsters were doing other things.

"They Never Gave Me My Testimony"

STEPHEN R. COVEY

Many people are very tender inside, very susceptible to the teachings and examples of people who embody the values they admire. They identify with these people. This is particularly the case in the Church. Because the Church is divine in origin and direction, many tend to assume that leaders within the Church, general as well as local, are a lot further along the path to perfection than in fact they are. They then build their security on such expectations and hopes and thereby become dependent and vulnerable. They can be terribly hurt and disillusioned when a particular leader, teacher, mentor, or hero of some kind "doesn't come through." They forget or do not understand that almost everyone has his Achilles' heel and therefore may not be able to measure up to the standard of perfection in every observed situation.

I used to work with the devotional program at Brigham Young University and in that capacity was involved in inviting General Authorities to come and speak. I became well acquainted with their dislikes, their likes, and their idiosyncrasies. One time I was visiting with President Marion G. Romney about this, and he half jokingly said, "Stephen, don't get so close to the Brethren that you lose your testimony."

In that same mood of the half jest, I responded, "Well, they never gave me my testimony; they couldn't take it away."

He was fully serious in his comeback. "That's right, and don't you ever forget it."

The Greater Sin

Spencer W. Kimball

I was struggling with a community problem in a small ward in the East where two prominent men, leaders of the people, were deadlocked in a long and unrelenting feud. Some misunderstanding between them had driven them far apart with enmity. As the days, weeks, and months passed, the breach became wider. The families of each conflicting party began to take up the issue and finally nearly all the people of the ward were involved. Rumors spread and differences were aired and gossip became tongues of fire until the little community was divided by a deep gulf. I was sent to clear up the matter. After a long stake conference, lasting most of two days, I arrived at the frustrated community about 6 P.M., Sunday night, and immediately went into session with the principal combatants.

How we struggled! How I pleaded and warned and begged and urged! Nothing seemed to be moving them. Each antagonist was so sure that he was right and justified that it was impossible to budge him.

The hours were passing—it was now long after midnight, and despair seemed to enshroud the place; the atmosphere was still one of ill temper and ugliness. Stubborn resistance would not give way. Then it happened. I aimlessly opened my Doctrine and Covenants again and there before me it was. I had read it many times in past years and it had had no special meaning then. But tonight it was the very answer. It was an appeal and an imploring and a threat and seemed to be coming direct from the Lord. I read from the seventh verse on, but the quarreling participants yielded not an inch until I came to the ninth verse. Then I saw them flinch, startled, wondering. Could that be right? The Lord was saying to us—to all of us—"Wherefore, I say unto you, that ye ought to forgive one another."

This was an obligation. They had heard it before. They had said it in repeating the Lord's Prayer. But now: ". . . for he that forgiveth not his brother his trespasses standeth condemned before the Lord . . ."

In their hearts, they may have been saying: "Well, I might forgive if he repents and asks forgiveness, but he must make the first move." Then the full impact of the last line seemed to strike them: "For there remaineth in him the greater sin."

What? Does that mean I must forgive even if my antagonist remains cold and indifferent and mean? There is no mistaking it.

A common error is the idea that the offender must apologize and humble himself to the dust before forgiveness is required. Certainly, the one who does the injury should totally make his adjustment, but as for the offended one, he must forgive the offender regardless of the attitude of the other. Sometimes men get satisfaction from seeing the other party on his knees and grovelling in the dust, but that is not the gospel way.

Shocked, the two men sat up, listened, pondered a minute, then began to yield. This scripture, added to all the others read, brought them to their knees. Two A.M. and two bitter adversaries were shaking hands, smiling and forgiving and asking forgiveness. Two men were in a meaningful embrace. This hour was holy. Old grievances were forgiven and forgotten, and enemies became friends again. No reference was ever made again to the differences. The skeletons were buried, the closet of dry bones was locked and the key was thrown away, and peace was restored.

$\mathcal{M}$y Priorities

Bette S. Molgard

O
ur son, McKay, turned fifteen about the time that I decided my season had shifted. He was our only child at home and has always been very independent. I was job sharing a second grade classroom and worked every morning from eight o'clock until noon after dropping McKay off at the high school. It was the perfect job, but my love and longings had always been in the medical field. Before I had married, I had taken the prerequisites for a career in that field, applied for acceptance, and, notwithstanding my high G.P.A., had not been accepted because I was engaged. (This was, of course, many years ago.) I transferred my credits to the university Max was attending. There was no choice in the medical field, but I was told I could have a science concentration filled and lose no credits if I transferred to elementary education. I reluctantly finished and after my children were in school, had been surprised at how much I enjoyed teaching.

Observing the miracle of birth as my granddaughter was born rekindled my interest in medicine. I love the delivery room and decided the time was right for me to pursue a nursing degree. After checking around, I found that the college Max commutes to every day to teach institute had a nursing program. They would accept all of the science classes I had already taken if I would just take pathophysiology to review anatomy and physiology. My long-ago excitement got percolating. I quit my teaching job and enrolled for fall quarter. The pathophysiology, chemistry, and nutrition classes that quarter would complete my prerequisites for the nursing program. The schedule necessitated five-days-a-week attendance, and it only made sense for me to go with Max. I added an institute class and instead of walking every day with my friend at home, I made new friends and started walking at 7 A.M. with my associates at the college. I showered and dressed at the physical education facility after walking and was ready for my 9 A.M. class. We would return home about five o'clock in the afternoon.

We had a long talk with McKay. He seemed to be the only one besides me who was affected by my new schedule, and he didn't seem to mind getting himself up and off to school; in fact, he encouraged it. Football practice usually prevented him from coming home to an empty house.

The opportunity to find out my brain still functioned above a second grade level was stimulating, and for the first time in a long time, I was spending a lot of hours with my husband. I relished our togetherness.

Despite the positive list, I became troubled shortly after the quarter started. McKay's attendance, grades, and attitude all took a turn for the worse. Our older children were patient but a bit disappointed that I had disappeared from their lives. I was not only unavailable during the school hours, but homework kept me occupied at night. I didn't have time to do family history, play with the grandchildren, or study effectively to teach my Gospel Doctrine class on Sunday.

The quarter was soon over, and during the long Christmas break I was accepted into the nursing program. It was time to take another look at my options. The full menu was available, but choosing to be a nurse eliminated so many highly valued parts of my life. Sister Janath R. Cannon informs us that "Richard L. Evans once remarked that some things were *only* worth doing if they didn't have to be done so well that they interfered with more important things" ("Priorities in the Pursuit of Excellence," *Ensign,* April 1976, p. 70). I spent several days and eventually one sleepless night pondering my priorities. My prayerful decision opened a spot in the nursing program.

I began to look for other possible ways to fill my wants without eliminating other needs. Our local hospital was looking for technicians to work in labor and delivery. They explained that the job, should I decide to accept it, would entail being on call for a twelve hour shift one day a week. I would more or less be a gopher for the doctor and nurses. There wouldn't be much money involved, but I would be in the delivery room and I wouldn't need any more schooling except specific training at the hospital. That choice made everything else fall into place as I filled the rest of the days of the week with all of the people and activities that were important to me.

My experience highlights how priorities work. We need to decide what is of most value and arrange our schedules around that.

"Tell Me How You Do It"

HUGH B. BROWN

This incident occurred in England in 1944. I had gone to England at the request of the First Presidency as co-ordinator for the L.D.S. servicemen. One Saturday afternoon I sent a telegram from London to the base chaplain of a certain area near Liverpool, saying, "I shall be in your camp tomorrow morning and shall appreciate your advising the Mormon boys who are there that we will have a service at ten o'clock."

When I arrived in that camp, there were seventy-five Mormon boys, all in uniform, and quite a number in battle dress. The chaplain to whom I had sent the wire proved to be a Baptist minister from the Southern States. He was waiting, too, for my arrival, and as these young men ran out to greet me, not because it was I, but because of what I represented, and as they literally threw their arms around me, knowing that I was representing their parents as well as the Church, this minister said to me: "Please tell me how you do it?"

"Do what?"

"Why," he said, "I did not get your wire until late this morning. I made a hurried search. I found there were seventy-six Mormon boys in this camp. I got word to them. Seventy-five of them are here. One is in the hospital. I have over 600 men of my church in this camp, and if I gave them six months' notice I could not get a response like that," and then he repeated, "Tell me how you do it."

I said, "Sir, if you will come inside, perhaps you will see." We went into the little chapel. The boys sat down. I asked "How many here have been on missions?"

I think fully 50 percent raised their hands. I said, "Will you and you and you," and I pointed to six of them, "come and administer the Sacrament? And will you and you and you," and I pointed to six others, "please come and sit here and be prepared to speak?"

Then I said, "Who can lead music?" A number of hands were raised. "Will you come and lead the music? And who can play this portable organ?" There were several hands, and one was selected. Then I said, "What would you like to sing, fellows?" And with one voice they replied, "Come, Come, Ye Saints."

We had no hymnbooks. The boy sounded the chord. They all arose. I have heard "Come, Come, Ye Saints" in many lands and by many choirs and congregations, and without in any way reflecting adversely on what we usually do and hear, I think I have only heard "Come, Come, Ye Saints" sung once when every heart seemed bursting, as they sang every verse without books. When they came to the last verse, they didn't mute it, they didn't sing it like a dirge, but throwing back their shoulders, they sang out until I was fearful that the walls would burst. "And should we die before our journey's through, happy day, all is well," and I looked at my minister friend and found him weeping.

Then one of the boys who had been asked to administer the Sacrament knelt at the table, bowed his head and said, "Oh, God, the Eternal Father;" he paused for what seemed to be a full minute, and then he proceeded with the rest of the blessing on the bread. At the close of that meeting I sought that boy out. I put my arm around his shoulders, and said, "Son, what's the matter? Why was it so difficult for you to ask the blessing on the bread?" He paused for a moment and said, rather apologetically, "Well, Brother Brown, it isn't two hours since I was over the continent on a bombing mission. As we started to return, I discovered that my tail assembly was partly shot away; that one of my engines was out; that three of my crew were wounded, and it looked like it was absolutely impossible to reach the shores of England. Brother Brown, up there I remembered Primary and Sunday School, and MIA, and home and church, and up there, when it seemed that all hope was lost, I said, 'O God, the Eternal Father, please support this plane until we reach a landing field.' He did just that, and when we landed, I learned of this meeting, and I had to run all the way to get here. I didn't have time to change my battle dress, and then when I knelt there and again addressed the Lord, I was reminded that I hadn't stopped to say thanks. Brother Brown, I had to pause a little while to tell God how grateful I was."

Well, we went on with our meeting. We sang. Prayers were offered, and these young men, with only a moment's notice, each stood and spoke, preached the gospel of Jesus Christ to their comrades, and bore their testimonies, and again I say with due respect to the various ones with whom I have associated and labored, they were among the finest sermons I ever heard. Then the time was up, and I said, "Fellows, it's time for chow. We must dismiss now or you will miss your dinner." And, again almost with one voice, they said, "We can eat army grub any time. Let's have a testimony meeting." So we stayed another hour and a half while every man arose and bore witness to the truth of the restored gospel of Jesus Christ, and each one in turn, in his own way, said, "I know that God lives; I know that the gospel is restored; I know that Joseph Smith was a Prophet of God." Again I looked at my friend, and he was weeping unashamedly.

At the close of that meeting this minister said to me, "I have been a minister for over twenty-one years, but this has been the greatest spiritual experience of my life." And again he said, "How do you do it?"

Then it was my pleasure to tell him about the Primary and the Sunday School and the MIA, with the various activities of the priesthood quorums, the seminaries, the Church schools, and the great educational system directed by the Church board of education through the faculty of Brigham Young University. I told him of our missionary system, of the training it provides, and the testimonies resulting from such gratuitous service.

This minister said to me, "If we could accomplish something like that among the young people of our Christian churches, there would be no more war. Why, I would not dare to call on members of my congregation to speak without a moment's notice. They who do come to church know that I am going to speak and that they have no responsibility. But here it seems every man is a minister, and every one has been trained to participate."

I explained to him that those men had been taking part since they were little tots, and I told him further, and I say to you, that that experience could have been, and was in many instances, repeated in various camps in the United States and Canada and Europe.

*Un*ity or Uniformity?

ANNE OSBORN POELMAN

The annual North America Central Area Mission Presidents' Seminar was approaching rapidly. This particular year the meeting was to be held under the direction of Elder Neal A. Maxwell. At the time, Ron, my husband, was serving in the Area Presidency and we were consequently both invited to attend the seminar in historic Nauvoo, Illinois.

Mission presidents' seminars, traditionally three-day events that include instructional, spiritual, and some recreational activities, are carefully planned and greatly anticipated by the leaders and their wives. Much prayerful, thoughtful consideration is given to both the content and structure of these important meetings.

All the participants, namely the General Authorities and their wives as well as the mission presidents and their wives, would attend plenary sessions of this conference. A special breakout session for the wives had also been included in the packed schedule. As wife of the presiding senior Apostle, Sister Colleen Maxwell was our designated leader. She was acutely conscious of her responsibilities as well as very much aware of the unique nature of our special meeting and the opportunities it presented.

Well in advance of the meeting, Sister Maxwell asked the other General Authorities' wives to meet with her and discuss ideas about the session. Several suggestions were offered that might maximize the meeting's effectiveness. As is nearly always the case, the number of potential discussion items far outweighed the relatively limited time allowed for them.

After hearing everyone out, Sister Maxwell began to assign responsibilities. I, the youngest and by far the least experienced member of the group, was greatly relieved when the program was nearly complete and my name hadn't been mentioned.

My relief didn't last.

"Annie," Sister Maxwell said, turning to me, "I think we should hear from you at the meeting."

I groaned inwardly but still hoped my participation might be a relatively simple assignment, something like giving the closing prayer.

No such luck. "In fact," she added, "the more I think about it, the more I feel you should lead the discussion period. You could take a few minutes at the beginning and then open the discussion up to everyone."

Oh, no! I thought. I had only attended two other mission presidents' seminars and knew that such an assignment required the wisdom of experience combined with a real feeling for the challenges the sisters faced on a daily basis.

"Colleen," I demurred, "you know I'll do whatever you ask. But I feel really strange about the whole thing. I'm a convert. I didn't grow up in the Church. I've never been on a mission. I've never had children. I know zip about teenagers. And I've never cooked for the masses, either! What in the world would I talk about? What could I say that anyone doesn't already know better than I do?"

Everyone chuckled at my discomfort.

Sister Maxwell was insistent. "Annie, we're putting you on the program for the discussion."

Later I spoke to her privately. "Are you sure about this?" I inquired dubiously.

She smiled, "I'm sure."

"What do you think we should discuss?"

"Frankly, I don't know."

"You don't know!" my panic rose a notch.

"No. But you will," she said gently but firmly.

I've never lost any sleep over giving medical lectures or delivering a scientific paper to an audience of thousands. But I experienced a lot of wakeful nights after Sister Maxwell's assignment. I prayed about it intensely and knew she was right. I was supposed to speak briefly and then lead the main discussion. On what topic, I hadn't the faintest idea.

I prayed about the specific subject and got no answer. There would be plenty of doctrinal discussions in the plenary sessions, and I didn't think more of the same would be appropriate.

Desperate for suggestions, I called several women I knew who had been mission presidents' wives. Some had interesting ideas but they just didn't seem quite right for us. I even thought of calling half a dozen women who were "old hands" and asking each one for her best two or three recipes to serve a minimum of twenty!

With barely a week left before the seminar, I had almost concluded this would have to be one of those times when "it shall be given you in that same hour what ye shall speak" (Matthew 10:19).

Then, quite suddenly and unexpectedly, the answer came.

The Midwest in late autumn is glorious. The suffocating heat and high humidity of summer have faded, yielding to pleasantly sunny days and cool, crisp evenings. Silos and corn cribs are filled to bursting with the rich harvest and the fertile, loamy fields are meticulously plowed and fertilized in anticipation of the next plantings. Produce stands spring up along country roads, offering pumpkins, Indian corn, assorted decorative gourds, late harvest pears, and homemade jams. The fall colors are past their peak, but a few leaves cling tenaciously to barren branches and brightly colored berries accent the dense underbrush.

We drove across the broad, lazy Mississippi River toward the Nauvoo lowlands. After freshening up at our hotel, we had a lovely dinner and retired early in anticipation of the next day's crowded schedule.

Ron and I arose before dawn to jog through the restored town and around the old temple site, then turned down along the river bank. The air was pungent, redolent with earthy odors and the damp smell of the nearby Mississippi. I would have enjoyed the spectacular dawn had I not felt so nervous. Mercifully, I didn't have an interminably long wait. The sisters' seminar was scheduled for the afternoon session of the first day.

The opening session was truly outstanding. Elder Maxwell presided and welcomed everyone. After the introductions he spoke briefly, then called on several members of the Area Presidencies (including Ron) to speak. Elder Maxwell then filled the balance of the morning with an extraordinarily inspiring talk about Joseph Smith. We sat spellbound as he expressed his deep love for Joseph Smith and delineated some of the Prophet's most profound doctrinal insights. Engrossed in the ideas Elder Maxwell was discussing so movingly, I temporarily forgot my nervous apprehension.

Lunch was over in a flash and the sisters started gathering for our breakout meeting. They were excited and upbeat as they chatted together prior to the afternoon session. I said little, wondering if what I had planned would really work.

The wives relaxed visibly as Sister Maxwell started the meeting, immediately putting everyone at ease with her gracious manner and approachable personality. A promising beginning.

After the opening hymn and prayer, Sister Maxwell and the wives of the other two Area Presidency members spoke. She then announced that the balance of the afternoon would be an open, informal discussion that she had asked me to lead after I made some brief introductory remarks. She told them a bit about me, then sat down.

I stood up, praying silently, *Lord, please let it work.*

"Sisters," I said, unable to keep the nervous tension from my voice, "when Sister Maxwell gave me this assignment, I had no idea what to do. I felt really inadequate. Who am I to be teaching you? You've all been members of the Church longer than I have. You know the scriptures and the doctrines. You've already been out in the mission field for periods varying from a few months to over two years. I've never even been on a mission myself."

I could see a few wordless protests forming. "No," I continued, "I have little experience as a General Authority's wife. Ron and I have been married for just six years. I've never had children. In fact, Ron tells me my theories of child-raising—based purely on abstract ideas and not one whit in practical experience—would curl your hair!"

They laughed and I felt better.

"I don't know beans about teenagers. I've never cooked for more than a dozen people in my life. What I'm really good at is diagnosing brain tumors and strokes, and I hope that will never be very useful for you. So I really pondered and prayed about what the Lord wanted us to discuss this afternoon. It took some time, but I feel I finally received the answer. I'd like to talk with you about discouragement, depression, and their malignant cousin, despair."

I could hear a sharp intake of breath as the sisters reacted to this unexpected turn. I continued, "We all feel discouraged from time to time. Such feelings are normal when our responsibilities seem overwhelming and unremitting. Personal resources are strained and feelings of inadequacy are exacerbated when the demands and expectations of others exceed our ability to meet them.

"Frankly, at first I felt really discouraged when Sister Maxwell gave me this assignment. I couldn't imagine what I could ever bring to this discussion that might be helpful. I thought and prayed about it. For a long time I didn't have the slightest clue. It made me feel inadequate, even a bit desperate. Maybe that's part of the process: learning to recognize our own shortcomings. Realizing our dependence on the Lord and somehow learning to cope with always falling short is another part."

I talked about the difference between feeling discouraged and being depressed. I then asked the sisters what they thought depression really was. How could it be recognized and helped? Did they know anyone who might be suffering from depression?

At first the sisters hesitated, each reluctant to be the first to comment. When one finally spoke up, the dam broke.

The afternoon flew by. When Ron opened the door to gather us for the closing session, the sisters were still talking animatedly. Realistically. Hopefully. And about a topic they had initially felt reluctant to discuss.

Those sisters felt good. I did too. My inexperience and different background hadn't been a handicap at all. In fact, it was okay, and safe, to express openly our feelings of inadequacy. To me that's one of the most wonderful things about the Church. Years later, I occasionally encounter some of those sisters. They still talk about that unusual session and how helpful it was in dealing with some of their missionaries.

That experience helped me recognize that each of us has a special, even unique role to serve in the kingdom. Uniformity is not necessary or even desirable; unity is. My life circumstances were very different from those of the mission presidents' and other General Authorities' wives. Yet our testimonies, firm commitment to the gospel, and dedication to the Lord's church united us.

The Apostle Paul stated, "Ye are all one in Christ Jesus" (Galatians 3:28). The Savior himself prayed to the Father that his apostles and all the saints "may be one, as we are" (John 17:11). The unity of which Jesus spoke does not require us to become identical. It does entreat us as individuals to be of one mind and purpose in our shared commitment to the kingdom.

Character AND Attitude

Putting Character Above Popularity

Janette Hales Beckham

My first husband, Robert H. Hales, who passed away in 1988, practiced medicine, and whenever he was asked to write a letter of recommendation for a student applying to medical school, he told them this experience that he had with one of his classmates.

As you know, it isn't easy to get into medical school, and as you would guess, freshman students are not only enthusiastic but are committed to very hard work. My husband said he still remembers going to his first examination at the University of Utah. The honor system was in place. As the professor passed out the examination and left the room, he said some classmates started to pull out little cheat papers from pockets and from under their books. He said, "My heart began to pound, and I realized how difficult it is to compete with cheaters." It appeared that this was a practice that must have been common in some settings in the past. About then a tall, thin student stood up in the back of the room and said, "I left my hometown and put my wife and three little children in an upstairs apartment to go to medical school, and I'll turn in the first one of you who cheats and YOU BETTER BELIEVE IT!" They believed it. My husband said he looked like Abraham Lincoln. There were many sheepish expressions, and those cheat papers started to disappear as fast as they had appeared. It's interesting that that class graduated the largest graduating class in the history of the school. That young man set a standard of hard work and cooperation instead of dishonesty. That man cared more about character than popularity. When I heard the name of J. Ballard Washburn to be sustained as a member of the Quorum of Seventy, I remembered that he was that medical student. Whether or not J. B. had been called to be a General Authority, I realized his name would have been known for good wherever he was. He developed character!

After relating this experience as he remembered it, my husband would say to the student, "If you will work to develop that kind of character, I will write the letter of recommendation for you."

"She Became an Angel"

STEPHEN R. COVEY

I remember speaking at an Education Week in Phoenix when a lady came up to talk to me about the speech I had given the previous year at an Education Week in California on the subject of being a light and not a judge. She related to me her story of the intervening year.

She began by identifying how depressed she had been the year previous because of the lack of valiance in her husband's lifestyle. He had never caught fire in the gospel or the Church and was just barely getting along. She however had been illuminated with the gospel light and wanted the full blessings of the Lord on her entire family. She had tried every method she had heard of in an effort to influence her husband, all without success; and she had eventually succumbed to depression and cynicism.

Hearing my previous presentation, she was temporarily stimulated by the idea that her calling was to be a light, not a judge—in other words, a constant producer of good attitudes and behavior rather than a critic of her husband's poor attitudes and behavior. (After all, where in all the scriptures are we counseled to confess another's sins?) She decided to try it. She did so, and for several weeks she had a very difficult time in maintaining this new course.

As an example, she recounted that one time when she was preparing to go to church with the children, none of whom was very enthusiastic to go, she asked her husband in the middle of the TV program if he would join her in going to church and would help her with the children. He said he didn't want to go, that he wanted to finish watching his television program, and added, "You should let the kids stay and watch it and not force them to go to church." She swallowed hard and remembered she was striving to be a light, not a judge; a model, not a critic. Normally she would snip at him at the end of the encounter by saying something like,

"Well, if these kids don't turn out right, you know whose fault it is"—then she would immediately leave, giving him no opportunity for a rejoinder. She always tried to get in the last word and couch it in the language of the scriptures. It was her way of getting some kind of justice.

This time, however, she said nothing as she left, but merely took the children along with her and drove to church. While driving, she condemned herself for not performing her traditional judgment act on her husband for his lack of valiance, and the withdrawal pains she experienced were severe. She was breaking a deeply impacted habit that was addicting to her—the habit of getting back, of justifying, of having the last word, of putting down. She persisted with this changed behavior, even though she experienced great internal emotional turmoil for several weeks. At one point she was about to abandon the entire project, but fortunately she counseled with her bishop. He encouraged her to keep it up, and she did.

At the Arizona Education Week she now pointed out her husband, who was across the hall, and said, "There's my husband. He is now a member of the bishopric." I asked her if she would mind if I talked with her husband regarding what had happened. She felt good about it and so did he, and he described the process.

He said he had felt completely justified in his relative lack of commitment to the gospel, because apparently there were no real, powerful fruits of it in her life. She wasn't really changed because of the gospel and the Church. Further, she would punish him from time to time in various ways, and that made him feel justified in his minor rebellions. She paid him off, and this gave him the "right" to do it some more. He even sensed her new method—be a light, not a judge—and her striving not to answer back or fight or yell or criticize. But he knew what she was really thinking and feeling inside, and to some degree he enjoyed her being punished, as she had been punishing him for such a long time.

At this point in his account he said something that struck me forcibly. "But she persisted until this new behavior became a habit to her, and I began to sense that she was changing inside also; she wasn't punishing or manipulating me any longer, and she derived no more satisfaction from the encounters." He added, "She became an angel, Brother Covey, and how do you live with an angel?"

Well, eventually you can't live with an angel unless you change to a like condition. You eventually shape up or ship out. Whatever good there is in one person is appealed to by the angelic nature of the other. Most people have a great deal of good within them, and if only others would perceive it and treat them accordingly, this would tend to bring it out.

The Parable of the Treasure-Vault

James E. Talmage

Neither the story nor its application is the invention of the author; only the telling is his.

Among [some] news items was the report of a burglary, some incidents of which are unusual in the literature of crime. The safety-vault of a wholesale house dealing in jewelry and gems was the object of attack. From the care and skill with which the two robbers had laid their plans it was evident that they were adept in their nefarious business.

They contrived to secrete themselves within the building, and were locked in when the heavily-barred doors were closed for the night. They knew that the great vault of steel and masonry was of the best construction and of the kind guaranteed as burglar-proof; they knew also that it contained treasure of enormous value; and they relied for success on their patience, persistence, and craft, which had been developed through many previous though lesser exploits in safe-breaking. Their equipment was complete, comprising drills, saws and other tools, tempered to penetrate even the hardened steel of the massive door, through which alone entrance to the vault could be effected. Armed guards were stationed in the corridors of the establishment and the approaches to the strong-room were diligently watched.

Through the long night the thieves labored, drilling and sawing around the lock, whose complicated mechanism could not be manipulated even by one familiar with the combination, before the hour for which the time-control had been set. They had calculated that by persistent work they would have time during the night to break open the safe and secure such of the valuables as they could carry; then they would trust to luck, daring, or force, to make their escape. They would not hesitate to kill if they were opposed. Though the difficulties of the undertaking were greater than had been expected, the skilled criminals succeeded with tools and explosives in reaching the interior of the lock; then they threw back the bolts, and forced open the ponderous door.

What saw they within? Drawers filled with gems, trays of diamonds, rubies, and pearls, think you? Such and more they had confidently expected to find and to secure; but instead they encountered an inner safe, with a door heavier and more resistant than the first, fitted with a mechanical lock of more intricate construction than that at which they had worked so strenuously. The metal of the second door was of such superior quality as to splinter their finely tempered tools; try as they would they could not so much as scratch it. Their misdirected energy was wasted; frustrated were all their infamous plans.

Like unto one's reputation is the outer door of the treasure-vault; like unto his character is the inner portal. A good name is a strong defense, but though it be assailed and even marred or broken, the soul it guards is safe, provided only the inner character be impregnable.

eroes

Edgar A. Guest

There are different kinds of heroes, there are
    some you hear about.
They get their pictures printed, and their names
    the newsboys shout;
There are heroes known to glory that were not
    afraid to die
In the service of their country and to keep the
    flag on high;
There are brave men in the trenches, there are
    brave men on the sea,
But the silent, quiet heroes also prove their
    bravery.

I am thinking of a hero that was never known
    to fame,
Just a manly little fellow with a very common
    name;
He was freckle-faced and ruddy, but his head
    was nobly shaped,
And he one day took the whipping that his comrades
    all escaped.
And he never made a murmur, never whimpered
    in reply;
He would rather take the censure than to stand
    and tell a lie.

And I'm thinking of another that had courage
    that was fine,
And I've often wished in moments that such
    strength of will were mine.
He stood against his comrades, and he left them
    then and there

When they wanted him to join them in a deed
    that wasn't fair.
He stood alone, undaunted, with his little head
    erect;
He would rather take the jeering than to lose
    his self-respect.

And I know a lot of others that have grown
    to manhood now,
Who have yet to wear the laurel that adorns the
    victor's brow.
They have plodded on in honor through the dusty,
    dreary ways,
They have hungered for life's comforts and the
    joys of easy days,
But they've chosen to be toilers, and in this their
    splendor's told:
They would rather never have it than to do some
    things for gold.

"Make It a Good Day!"

ELAINE CANNON

I stood on the corner with a teenage boy who was blind. He paused a moment and then stepped into the traffic. I cautioned him to wait until the light changed. Hearing me speak, he turned my way and smiled broadly: "Oh, thank you. With this wind blowing, it's hard to hear the cars coming. We've been trained to listen to the traffic pattern since we can't see the semaphores."

And knowing I was there, he began a friendly visit which lasted until we reached the blind center a block away. He told me he had lost his sight at age eight when he had been struck across his eyes with a ball bat. There had been months into years of tears and despair while a little boy learned to adjust to a terrible personal tragedy.

"How have you finally come to such a positive outlook?" I asked.

"One day my father was helping me fly my kite, and it became caught in the tree. When he finally got it for me, I was terribly upset because it was broken; and I cried out to my father over and over again, 'Fix it!' 'Fix it!' But he could not. He moved my hands across the torn paper and the splintered wood, the tangled string. 'It cannot be fixed, son,' my father said. 'Like your eyes, it cannot be fixed.' And suddenly I knew it was hopeless. I really couldn't fly my kite anymore. We'd have to do something else. And in that same moment I knew I'd never see again. I'd have to get along without sight. I guess I grew up then. Well, here I am—I can tell by the stones especially pebbling the walk in front of the center. Thanks, and make it a good day!"

Such wisdom from one so young and so handicapped is wisdom we can surely take to heart. There are some things we can do something about, like making it a good day no matter what, and some things we just have to accept and adjust to. And we ought to be making a good day of it with the time we have.

The Positives Approach

Joseph L. Bishop

Tracking positives," or reinforcing positive behavior and ignoring the negative, is the fastest way to change someone's behavior. This concept became very clear to me some years ago when I was a member of a consulting team contracted to assist in the training of personnel in a large well-known company in Chicago, Illinois. During the few days we were there it became obvious that there was a great deal of dissatisfaction with one of the receptionists. It was obvious why everyone unanimously wanted her services terminated. She was lazy and belligerent and lacking in skills, capacity, and tact. It seemed as if she went out of her way to cause problems.

The company was particularly concerned because this secretary represented the management's first attempt to employ unqualified people from minority groups and to help them develop their skills and talents through inservice training. One of the tasks given to us was to help that young lady become a competent secretary. Some jokingly referred to the project as "Mission Impossible."

One day this secretary, whom we will call Mary, received a telephone message for one of the salesmen. It was not uncommon for her to pay little attention to such messages, but on this occasion she did note the telephone number of the calling client. She did not write down the name of the salesman for whom the message was taken, however, nor the company that the client represented. Even the date was forgotten. The telephone message was not given to the salesman but was carelessly cast aside to finally end up trampled on the floor. It was only by accident that the salesman noticed it as he was passing by Mary's desk.

Picking it up, he recognized the telephone number of his most important client and immediately telephoned to see if he could be of service. Imagine his surprise to find out that the company had decided to upgrade all of the computer equipment in their large plant; and because the salesman had not returned their call, they assumed that he was not interested and had therefore made the decision to buy from a competitor.

The salesman tried desperately to assure the company that he was indeed interested. He insisted that if they would but give him time, he would do, free of charge, a complete needs analysis for their projected equipment upgrade. Finally, after much persuasion the company agreed to give him time to assess their future needs and submit a proposal. After many days of nearly round-the-clock work, the salesman was successful. His proposal was accepted by the company, and he was rewarded with a handsome bonus from his own company for his hard work.

It was at this point that he came to us. He insisted that Mary be discharged. Her sloppy work habits had nearly cost him his largest account, he argued. Not only had she neglected all of the pertinent information on the telephone message, but more importantly had failed to give it to him at all. Had he not noticed it on the floor, he would surely have lost his best and largest client. He maintained that her attitude was not only a detriment to him but to the whole company. He was determined that she be fired.

We asked him to try one last experiment with us. We explained to him the importance of helping her to change her attitude and the process of reinforcing positive actions and ignoring negative ones. We reviewed step by step everything that had occurred. The only positive act that we could identify was that she had, in fact, taken the telephone message. Clearly, the message as taken was not as complete as we would have desired, and she did not follow through. But after all, she had taken the message, and we had to identify a positive act.

We now asked the salesman to go to the nearest florist and buy her some flowers. He rebelled. He was not going to give her a gift for having nearly lost for him his most important client. We prevailed, and finally he did as requested.

He returned from the florist with a single long-stem rose in an attractive, small white vase. He presented it to her with a note that read: "To Mary, Because you took the time to record that particular message, I was able to make a large sale. Thank you. Bill."

What effect did this little act of kindness have upon Mary? All of a sudden she started taking down every telephone message that came in. She made certain that each was received by the appropriate salesman. Clearly, she enjoyed being rewarded with kindness. Her belligerent attitude was a defense mechanism to cover up her fear of failing. The salesmen, in turn, recognized the change in her attitude and responded accordingly. When she did something right, they complimented her on her work. Her supervisor pointed out to her that the letter she had typed last week had fourteen errors but that her latest letter had only seven. He noted that if she continued to progress at that rate, he would have no other option but to request a pay increase for her.

Mary started to have a better self-image. Her dress and general attitude improved as if overnight. And it all occurred because someone ignored all of the negative aspects and focused only on her positive qualities. In the beginning all had agreed that there were no positive aspects about her at all. As she progressed, it was as if everyone was pulling for her to succeed. Everyone took joy in her progress. Everyone participated in her advancement.

Some few years later I was in New York City on business. While there I decided to call upon my old friend who was the director of the training center wherein I had been a consultant. He had now risen to the rank of executive vice-president of that large and important company. I was directed from floor to floor until I finally arrived at the top floor of the skyscraper. I found myself in a roomy, very expensively decorated executive suite.

Soon a very attractive young lady came to personally accompany me into the inner office of my successful friend. He greeted me with affection. Then turning to his executive secretary, he said, "You remember Mary, don't you?" I could hardly believe my eyes. Could this attractive young lady possibly be the same girl who, a few short years earlier, was the least likely to succeed? She laughed warmly and said, "I wondered if you would remember me." It was indeed the same young woman. She was immaculately dressed, and self-assurance emanated from her very being.

She fit well into the corporate environment. She obviously was well respected. Her poise and good manners were exemplary. My friend later told me that he had never had such an outstanding and competent executive secretary. In every aspect she was superior.

The Lord rarely calls any of us for what we are, but rather for what we can become. The same environment of love and support which caused Mary to grow can do the same for you and others. The capacity and potential is there. It only needs development, as the Lord stated, by persuasion, long-suffering, gentleness, meekness, love unfeigned, kindness, and pure knowledge, without hypocrisy and without guile. These are the ingredients of successful interpersonal relations. Positive response to appropriate behavior brings forth positive results. Love begets love. It is a law. Bringing to light negative behavior by magnifying it also provokes negative results unless: 1) reproving with sharpness is done only when moved upon by the Holy Ghost, and 2) the one reproving shows forth afterwards an *increased* love, "lest he esteem thee to be his enemy."

$\mathcal{S}$occer Practice

MARILYNNE TODD LINFORD

$\mathbf{E}$very year I experience some depression around the end
of August. The summer demands more, physically and emotion-
ally, than the school year. I love having the children at home, but
I get tired. On one of these last-of-summer days I had been in the
car from 6:30 A.M. to 7:30 P.M. I had one last errand for the day—
to pick up John from soccer practice. I drove to the field to find
out I had arrived thirty minutes early. My frustration level was
high. What was I to do with thirty more minutes in the car? But then
a little voice seemed to say, "Aw, come on. Enjoy the moment."

I looked around to see if there was anything to enjoy—I
doubted there was. It was a familiar sight. The coach had divided
the boys into teams—skins and shirts. They were playing a game
on half the field, with only one goal and one goalie. I had seen it
all many times. But then I noticed George, the coach, who was
about twenty-seven, recently married, around six foot four, and
probably 250 pounds. My attention focused on an animated
George. He slapped his thighs and yelled, "Great block, Cory!" He
jumped up and spun around in an aerial three-sixty as a goal was
scored. He gleefully asked, "Hey, John, where were you when we
needed a goal on Saturday?" George hugged his wife as Colin, the
goalie, like a horizontal arrow, blocked a goal. "What a save,
Colin! What a save!" He laughed, danced, jumped, ran, complimented, smiled, cajoled. He was completely alive in this moment
in time.

In the few minutes I watched George, he laughed more than
I had in the whole year. He was filled. He was charged up and in
charge. His passion for life was contagious. I saw the boys
responding, laughing, high-fiving, playing soccer with energy and
skill—pleasing George and themselves. Then I looked beyond
the field where these few boys were practicing soccer. I saw

thick, green lawn, a school, children playing, houses, mountains, the sun saying farewell to the day. I saw the night coming and the stars beginning their job of giving light to the night. I saw myself suddenly happy, content, blessed to be alive and part of an orderly, splendid world.

I bowed my head and tears dropped to my shirt. I gave thanks.

Climbing Mt. Olympus

George D. Durrant

In the early 1980s, one of my New Year's resolutions was to climb Mt. Olympus, the nine-thousand-foot mountain that rises high above the Salt Lake Valley floor.

My eleven-year-old son Mark and I arose at five o'clock in the morning to make the climb. It was still pitch dark as we began to walk down the rough road that leads along the side of the mountain to the point where the trail begins. We had not gone more than a hundred yards when I tripped over an unseen rock. Despite my efforts to keep from falling, I twisted my ankle and fell forward to the hard earth. Mark, wondering what had happened, was greatly concerned. As I lay there on the ground, my ankle felt uncomfortably injured. I knew that I now had an excuse to give up and return home to bed, and that idea seemed to be my best chance for having my best day so far.

With some effort I was able to stand up. I decided to try to walk. As I did so, I found that the pain seemed to subside. I thought I'd try to go a little further. I didn't tell Mark that there was some doubt about whether we would continue. After walking for several more minutes, my ankle felt increasingly better even though I could tell that it was slightly swollen.

The light in the eastern sky grew as we made our way up the rocky road. Soon the hill steepened. I had somehow thought that we could get to the top of the mountain without ever going uphill. As my breathing began to be more pained, I realized that to get from where we were to where we were going was going to be a struggle. The switchback trail led us higher and higher. I began to wish my ankle would hurt more so that I could have a legitimate reason to return home.

We crossed a small stream and started up a steep hill. The surface was more like a creek bed than a trail. I thought, "I can't make it to the top, but I'm going to keep going just a little bit further." Young Mark, who seemed to have unlimited energy, was willing to rest as often as I needed to. His greatest hope seemed to be that I would not give up.

Now the trail seemed to head directly into the sky. After several steps my heart pounded within my chest, and I sat gasping for breath. Then, after a few minutes, I had the strength to go on. Mark never seemed to tire.

We climbed higher and higher. I kept thinking that we'd soon be to a place where the trail would level off, but it didn't. Upward and upward we went. My strenuous efforts were paying off, and I said to Mark, "Well, we've done pretty good even if we don't make it to the top." He quickly let me know that he thought we could go all the way.

His enthusiasm and desire caused me to forge ahead twenty yards. Then I sat down and panted. We each took a tiny drink of water from our canteen and continued on. By now, I found myself wanting more and more to make it all the way to the top. But at the same time, I thought that perhaps before we could get there, I'd collapse.

After much stopping, catching breath, and forcing myself on, we came to a grove of pine trees that were a considerable distance up the mountain. We had supposed that we would arrive at the top by noon. However, by eleven we were still far from that point. Many thoughts went through my mind. I wondered why I was doing what I was doing. My only hope came from the feeling that even though my body was about to give up, my spirit seemed to be soaring higher and higher.

The top of the mountain gradually seemed to be getting reachable. But then the slope became steeper. I felt there was no way I could keep going. I'd go again for twenty yards, sit down and gasp and wonder if the wise thing to do would be to give up, while Mark, sensing my desire to surrender, would say with conviction, "We can make it, Father." I'd believe him. I'd struggle to my feet and up we'd go.

We had one backpack, and I was carrying it. I finally told Mark, "I can't carry this." He said he would. I could scarcely contain my joy when the trail leveled off and we were in another grove of pines. The noonday sun bore down on my sweat-drenched, weary body. Off to the south I saw a lesser peak. I knew we could get there without a great deal more effort. I asked Mark, "Is that the one we want to go to?" He replied, "No, that's not the one we said we'd climb." I knew even before he had spoken that we weren't going to go in that direction. Instead, we each looked to our left where the highest peak looked down at us.

We started up the rocks. Now it was a matter of pulling ourselves up large boulders. Mark went first. I had to stay off to the side as rocks were falling down. The top was now only a short way away. I felt a surge of pure hope. But just as I thought we had it made, the way became the most difficult of all. I pulled myself up one rock after another. We wound our way through chasms between giant boulders. It took us another half an hour to go only a short way, because I had to rest so often. Mark, sensing we were nearly there, could wait for me no longer. He ran ahead and shouted back, "Father, I'm here and it's beautiful!" He hurried back and led me forward. Finally, completely out of energy, I was at the top of Mt. Olympus.

No one had to tell me then why men climb mountains. The exhilaration of looking down at the valley and knowing that I had made it gave me a sense of satisfaction that I had seldom known before. My dear son and I had made it and we were together on top of the world. It was good to be where we said we'd be.

After this joyous time of savoring both our victory and the glorious view, we started our descent. In about half an hour we had made it back down the steepest portion. My ankle didn't hurt anymore, but I could tell that it was swollen considerably.

The sun was bearing down on us with all its fervor. It had been a warmer day than had been predicted. I was using different muscles in my legs now than those I had used on the way up, and those muscles were beginning to give out. My legs were becoming rubbery.

On and on Mark walked and I staggered. About a third of the way down, I picked up some speed and my foot caught fast under a protruding root. My momentum carried me forward, and even though my foot came free from the root I started to fall. It must have taken me ten yards before I finally hit the earth. Rocks dug into the palm of my hand as I tried to break the fall. Mark, seeing me fly toward him, quickly stepped aside and watched me as I sprawled to a landing. I wasn't really sure that I could get up. But there was no choice—I had to get up, so I did.

The steeper part was yet to come. I had to hold onto limbs along the way to keep from falling. I had serious doubts now that I could make it. I could envision a helicopter coming up to get me.

Down we continued. Finally, we came to the point where we had to go slightly uphill. It felt good to go uphill. I thought, "George, uphill is hard, but it's when you're going downhill in life that the pain becomes the greatest."

The ground leveled out. Mark was several yards ahead of me, and I could tell he was becoming impatient. Finally, I told him, "You just take off now and head for home. I'll come along soon." I knew then that the hardest part was over, even though it was desperately difficult to get one foot in front of the other.

Soon I saw there was only about a mile to go—a level mile. As I walked along, I was so grateful that I was nearly back. Hope welled up again in my heart. Finally, I was home. I was so thrilled to be home.

Later that day I attended an early evening meeting at our chapel. Every muscle in my body ached. I could hardly walk. My face was sunburned. After that meeting I went out and looked up at Mt. Olympus. It looked different now that I knew I had been to the top. I was so deeply proud of what I had done. I sensed then that a man was standing at my side. He asked, "What are you looking at?"

I said, "Mt. Olympus."

Then, in an almost bragging way, I said, "I've been to the top of that today."

He said, "Oh, really! That's great." Then he added, "I've been up there eighteen times."

"Eighteen times," I said. "Boy, that's really something."

He said, "Which way did you go—the easy way up back?"

I said, "Well, we went up back."

He said, "That's the easy way." After a brief pause, he continued, "I go right up the face." I kept gazing up. Suddenly I realized that what I had done was no major accomplishment for anybody else, but it was only a major accomplishment for me.

I thoughtfully turned and limped away. I wasn't in competition with him or anyone else. I was only in competition with myself, and today I had been a winner. And that made me say to myself, *"This has been my best day so far."* In the days and weeks that followed, I would look up at the lofty peak of Mt. Olympus and think, "I've been up there. Not to that lesser peak off to the right, but to that higher one—the top one—the one we said we'd climb and we did." Even now when I see majestic Mt. Olympus, I'm filled with the reward of that climb again and I say to myself, "I'm sure glad I didn't turn back."

Even though the day that I climbed Mt. Olympus was a great day, today is far better because today there is a new mountain to climb. Each day's mountain is different, but each day has within its hours a special mountain for each of us to climb. Today's mountain may be an upward slope through forests of fear, climbing under the hot sun of tedious tasks or across sheer boulders of my own expectations. Or it may be down a painful slope strewn with the loose and slippery rocks of selfishness or the entangling roots of pride.

But though sometimes I must rest and gasp for emotional breath, I must move forward. And though the downward momentum of unfulfilled hope may slam me to the ground, I must get up and go on to my goal.

Just as my son told me, "No, Dad, that lesser cliff is not our goal," so God's Son, in my greatest need, speaks to my soul and says, "No, not the lesser goal of compromise, but the lofty goal of fulfillment." So on I go, and as I do so today truly becomes my best day so far.

"*I* Can't Sing This"

RANDAL A. WRIGHT

hile attending a youth conference in a southern state, I listened as several youth bore their testimonies. Michelle, a beautiful African-American girl, walked up to the podium and told of her life's goal to be a recording artist and of the events that had recently happened in the pursuit of this goal.

She said that she had worked hard and that it finally appeared as if her dream would come true. Representatives from a recording company came to her home with a song and offered her the opportunity to make her first recording. Michelle felt like jumping up and down, she was so excited. But then she began reading the words to the song that had been written for her, and a sick feeling came over her. She felt her newfound dream slipping away. The lyrics were not up to Church standards. They weren't too bad, but she didn't feel good about performing something that went against her values and beliefs.

There was silence in the room, and then Michelle looked up at the recording company representatives and said, "I can't sing this song. Its words go against what I believe in." The people tried to convince her that one song wouldn't matter. Michelle knew what she felt, but it hurt. After all, this was the big opportunity she had been waiting for.

But some things in life cannot be bought. Michelle stood up for what she knew was right. The answer was no. She could not and would not sing that song. The representatives left, and Michelle went to her room and cried herself to sleep. But she felt good that she had the courage to stand up for what was right.

Two days later someone knocked at Michelle's front door. There stood the same people who had visited her before. They explained that they had changed the lyrics just for her and that they still wanted her to sing it. This young woman, who stood up for what was right even when circumstances and those around her encouraged her to compromise her standards, now has her first recording out and will probably have many more to come. But more important, she knows the joy that comes from doing what is right.

$\mathscr{H}$e Would Not Give In

Joseph L. Bishop

There existed in the Church a mission that was considered "hard" by most of those who were called to serve there. All of the statistical reports of that mission confirmed those judgments. As new missionaries arrived, they were informed by the others that "this mission was not a high baptizing mission." When the new missionary heard such utterances, he almost always accepted it automatically, without question, and the mission continued on at the established level of low performance.

Elder Michaels arrived in that mission. Prior to his call he had often gone out with the full-time missionaries. He knew their programs and knew their trials, but most of all he knew their attitude. Those missionaries had a positive frame of mind. If they came up against an obstacle, they used it as a stepping-stone. There was an entirely different prevailing attitude in his home mission.

As Elder Michaels listened to the negative expressions of his new companions, he resolved that he would not allow them to affect his efforts. Until he found out on his own that the mission was indeed "impossible," as it was often referred to, he would not give in.

He found himself alone. His senior companion was soon to go home and was one of the head protagonists in keeping up the negative image of the mission. "The mission is hard," he proclaimed; therefore, "there's little use in trying." He went through the motions but did little else.

Elder Michaels was frustrated by his companion's attitude, but he did not give in to the insistent propaganda. His positive attitude remained intact. Soon he was the companion to a relatively new missionary who had not been totally conditioned into believing that the mission was impossible. They decided they would take the responsibility upon themselves to change the attitude of the mission by proving the other missionaries wrong. They knew that the Lord could use them to find, teach, and baptize his people and were determined to do so.

The hours were long and their bodies tired, but little by little they were able to build a pool of investigators. Then the baptisms began. These missionaries knew that for the Lord nothing is impossible. They trusted in him and in his power.

As families were baptized, these new members became interested in sharing the gospel with their friends and relatives. The Lord again poured forth his blessings. At first the missionaries were baptizing once every three months. Soon they were baptizing every month, and finally, they were baptizing nearly every week. At one point Elder Michaels and his companion were baptizing nearly one-third of all of the converts in the entire mission.

Hard mission? Mission Impossible? Or only the results of a negative attitude?

Missionaries should have faith that the Lord will bless them if they are righteous. They should have faith that there is nothing impossible for the Lord. They should go forth with the power of their convictions expressed in action and in a positive attitude—that is the driving force that will persuade men and women to repent and be baptized. The missionary who, with a positive attitude, cries out for all to hear, "I know that the Lord lives; I know Joseph Smith was a prophet; I know the Book of Mormon to be the word of God; I know that you can know it too"—that missionary will be blessed beyond measure.

The Roller-Skating Incident

Matthew Richardson

My father always stressed integrity in our home. As a matter of fact, his trademark was his personal integrity. I listened to the stories, morals, and lessons my father taught our family as I was growing up. More important, my father never gave me reason to doubt that his practice was not in harmony with his teachings. Like my father, my mother believed in integrity, but it was my father who seemed to talk about it. It was almost as if this was "Dad's thing." I learned the importance of integrity, however, through witnessing the partnership of my father and mother.

When I was in seventh grade, I was elected president of my class. After the announcement of the new class officers, some of the other elected officers mentioned to me that they were all going roller-skating that night at the local skating rink in celebration. Excited to be part of the new group, I immediately accepted their invitation. Later that evening, as I was waiting for my ride to the roller-skating rink, my mother reminded me of a birthday party I had previously committed to attend. Without telling my mother about the roller-skating celebration, I decided to go roller-skating rather than attend the birthday party.

Not long after we arrived at the skating rink, an announcement was made for all the girls to go to one side of the rink and all the boys to go to the opposite side. It was time for the "snowball," an activity in which one boy and one girl would skate to the opposite end of the rink and choose a partner to skate with. At the cue, the couples would break and each would then choose another partner. This would continue until it "snowballed" into a large group with everyone skating. I must admit it sounds rather childish, but to a seventh grader this was high adventure! After the rules were explained over the loudspeakers, the houselights were dimmed and the mirror ball began spinning, casting spots throughout the rink. As we waited for the music to begin, I saw a silhouetted figure walking across the floor. Since this person was not wearing skates, I thought it must be the manager coming out to start the activity. This person didn't walk like a manager, however, but more like a person on a mission: leaning slightly forward, taking purposeful steps, and moving fast. As this figure came closer, I realized that it wasn't the manager of the skating rink. To my horror, I realized that it was my mother!

Almost in military cadence, my mother marched right up to me, grabbed me by my arm, and said, "Come with me, young man!" I was familiar enough with my mother's vocabulary to know that anytime you were called by your full name or addressed as "young man," you were in serious trouble. She marched me across the roller-skating rink and sat me down on a bench. "Change your skates," she said. "We're leaving." I hurriedly changed into my shoes and was promptly escorted out of the rink, flushed with embarrassment. I had never been more mortified in all my twelve years of life! Didn't my mother realize that these were my new friends? Didn't she understand that popularity was a fragile venture? Did she know that she had just ended my prospects for any semblance of a normal seventh grade experience?

We didn't speak as she drove. I just looked out the window and grunted occasionally so she would know how upset I was. Rather than driving home, my mother drove straight to the birthday party I had originally committed to attend. She handed me a gift, reminded me to be a gentleman, and told me to get out of the car and go to the party. I was shocked. This was so embarrassing! Right before I slammed the car door shut, I told my mother that I would never speak to her again.

After the party, I walked home. As I walked into the house, my parents were sitting at the kitchen table. In silence I strode past them and went straight to my bedroom. As I lay in bed, I knew my parents were probably beside themselves questioning whether Mom's actions were appropriate or not. Maybe they were crying and lamenting that they had disjointed my young social life and scarred me for eternity. Now that I am a parent, when I reflect back on that experience I realize that my parents were probably giggling themselves silly as my mom told my father the whole story. By the way, I did speak to my mother again the very next morning—after all, I was hungry!

In time I began to realize something important about that experience. Whereas I once had been mortified by my mother's actions, I learned to cherish her decision. Of course, I came to understand the error in my judgment of not honoring my previous commitment to the birthday party. My father's lessons and examples made that clear; all I could think of was, "My word is my bond." It was the combination of my father's lessons and my mother's determined raid of Rollercity that forever riveted the importance of integrity onto my soul. I knew my father and mother were united and that their partnership was lasting. Integrity wasn't just my father's hobby; it was my parents' value. The experience of witnessing their partnership in power has forever altered my life. I am indebted and grateful to have learned such important principles at such an early age.

Home AND Family

A Kiss from Dad

George D. Durrant

My son was on the high school basketball team. At one point the coach advised the team members that he didn't think they were all doing as much as they should to be ready for the forthcoming tournament. He asked them all to make some special sacrifice with that in mind.

My son and some of the others decided that their sacrifice would be to get up early each morning and go over to school and practice basketball before school started. One morning while he was in the midst of this program I got up as early as he did so as to cook him breakfast. (His mother had had a broken sleep, and since it was now very early she remained in bed.)

We happened to have some bacon in the fridge. I cooked a lot more of it than I would have been able to had his mother been up. I fried him a few eggs. I made him some toast. I made him a drink by mixing some ice, some milk, some chocolate and a little ice cream. It was kind of a "good morning" milk shake. I had my son sit down at the table, then I served it all to him as if he were a king.

As he ate we talked. The only time my children have ever really talked to me is when I've been with them. He was most gracious as we talked, and we had a choice time together—just a father and son in that kitchen. When the food was all gone (and that wasn't long, the way he ate), it was time for him to go. He announced, "I've got to go quick, Pops" (that's what he calls me).

"Couldn't you just stay for a minute longer," I asked, "just long enough for you and me to kneel down and have a word of prayer?"

He could have said, "No, I've got to hurry," or he could have been ornery about it. But instead he quickly said: "Sure, Pops. There's always time for that."

He knelt down, and I knelt as close as I could to him. I acted as the voice for our prayer. I told Heavenly Father how grateful I was to have such a son. And in my prayers I poured out quite a few sentimentalities as I told the Lord how deeply I appreciated the way this young man was living and the things he was doing. I said so many things that the prayer was a rather long one. But he was patient and didn't seem to be fidgety, so I prayed on and on until I finally said amen.

After the prayer we both stood up. The Spirit of the Lord was present and my heart was filled with joy. I felt impressed to embrace my son and give him a kiss on the cheek. I don't do that often, but at that moment I just felt compelled to do it. Sensing what was happening, he didn't quickly take a karate stance as he could have done. Instead he embraced me and allowed me to kiss him on the cheek. As I did so I said, "Sure love ya." He looked at me with kind of a grin on his face and he said, "Sure love you, Pops." Then he turned and went towards the door.

Just as he was about to close the door, he looked back and grinned again. He almost laughed as he goodnaturedly said, "Gee, Pops, I wonder how many other Provo High basketball players got a kiss from their dad before they went to school this morning?" I told him to get out of there or he would get something more than just a kiss—a kick in the pants. He laughed and hurried away. I watched him from the window until he was gone from sight. Oh, how I felt my love for him that morning!

Only a Dad

EDGAR A. GUEST

Only a dad with a tired face,
Coming home from the daily race,
Bringing little of gold or fame
To show how well he has played the game;
But glad in his heart that his own rejoice
To see him come and to hear his voice.

Only a dad with a brood of four,
One of ten million men or more
Plodding along in the daily strife,
Bearing the whips and the scorns of life,
With never a whimper of pain or hate,
For the sake of those who at home await.

Only a dad, neither rich nor proud,
Merely one of the surging crowd,
Toiling, striving from day to day,
Facing whatever may come his way,
Silent whenever the harsh condemn,
And bearing it all for the love of them.

Only a dad but he gives his all,
To smooth the way for his children small,
Doing with courage stern and grim
The deeds that his father did for him.
This is the line that for him I pen:
Only a dad, but the best of men.

"Don't Forget, Mom"

Karen J. Ashton

Sometimes it takes time to see the humor in a situation, particularly when you're the one who makes the mistake. My son Morgan was chosen to be Santa Claus in his first grade Christmas program. Such an honor! I was eight months pregnant with our eighth child and had my hands full with two little preschoolers. I stayed up until 2:00 A.M. sewing his costume. As he ran out to the bus stop the next morning, he yelled, "Don't forget, Mom. The program is at 1:00."

I replied, "Me forget? Never! I wouldn't miss it for anything. You're going to be the best Santa ever. I can't wait to hear your Ho Ho Ho."

At eleven o'clock I put my two preschoolers down for a nap. I thought, "If I'm lucky, they might sleep until twelve." I woke up at 1:20! By the time I got to the school with my two little ones in tow there were no cars in the parking lot. Bad sign! When I reached the school library, Morgan was sitting alone on a chair in the middle of the room. All the other mothers had taken their children home right after the program. His little body was slumped forward. The Santa beard I had made the night before was hanging from one hand. His eyes were trained on his little black boots. The thought that I had inflicted pain on my own son stabbed at me. Kneeling in front of his chair I broke into tears. I pleaded with him to forgive me. I told him it had been a terrible mistake. He turned away from me. Great sobs now shook my body. One of my little preschoolers started patting my back in an attempt to comfort me. Suddenly, I could hear someone else in the room crying. It was Morgan's teacher. She begged him to forgive me. He only turned further away. Finally, when there were no more tears, I stood, gathered my preschoolers and Morgan's backpack, and started out to the car. Luckily he followed. There was no laughing that day.

Years later Morgan was running for high school student body vice president. We stayed up night after night working on posters, assemblies, and campaign buttons as well as entertaining fellow candidates. On the night that the election results were to be announced, both of us were exhausted. He left early for a candidate dinner. I refused to take a nap for fear I would miss the announcement dance.

Later that evening my husband and I sat on the high school bleachers waiting. As each new officer was announced, a cheer arose from the students assembled. The new officer would then come to the front and accept his position. Finally it was time. The speaker blared out, "Vice President for 1991—Morgan Ashton!" Everyone cheered. Morgan did not come to the front. Three times they called his name. I was sick! Where could he be? Suddenly, I knew.

My husband and I drove home and I ran downstairs to his room. When I opened the door I could see two big feet sticking out from the bottom of the bed. He had slept through the announcement. Apparently he had come home after the dinner and slipped downstairs for a little nap. I shook his foot, "You won, Morgan. You won!"

He groaned, then bolted upright. "No! No! I didn't miss it!"

"I'm so sorry," I said sincerely. "It was wonderful. Everyone cheered for you . . . three times."

Now he was really awake and in agony. "Oh, no!" He groaned.

I felt so sad for him. I confess, however, that images of his first grade program were dancing through my mind.

"There is something I need you to know," I said.

"What?" he asked.

Relieved, after *years* of guilt, I proudly stated, "I WAS THERE!"

I really do believe that sooner or later a mother who is doing her best has the last laugh.

Grandpa

RAND PACKER

Grandpas are meant to be. They are part of the plan that affects positively the growth of a young boy and provides him with some delicate direction that a father sometimes is unable to give.

One early September morning Dad loaded us kids into an old army-surplus open-bed jeep, and we headed for the mountain peaks far above our hometown. Shortly before entering the jeep trail that would take us to the summit, we heard the honking of a horn behind us and turned to see the familiar orange Oldsmobile that could mean only one thing: Grandpa had come to go with us. What a treat for us to have Dad and Grandpa for the entire day! Grandpa joined Dad in the front seat and off we went. It was fun to see them together, as they were cut from the same mold. From a distance they were impossible to tell apart, except that Grandpa's head glistened a little more on top than Dad's.

We stopped at the place where the river curled around, and we hiked for a while with Grandpa. He always checked the river for the size of fish and the prospective fishing holes for the future. Grandpa, an expert fisherman, had just retired and he was going to do a lot of fishing now.

Farther up the road we approached a rather sharp turn to the right. As we entered the turn, an old school bus converted into a camper entered the curve from the other direction. The bus loomed ominously before us, and its length required it to take our share of the road in order to negotiate the turn. With no time to stop or space to move over, Dad guided the jeep as best he could along the soft edge of the mountain road. We balanced precariously in the shifting dirt as the willows on the side tried desperately to keep us upright. But the jeep was too heavy, and over we went to the river below. Everyone was thrown clear except Grandpa and me.

Driven by frantic cries for help, my brother somehow found my right tennis shoe and pulled me out from under the jeep to safety. But Grandpa was not so fortunate. The jeep had pinned him underneath. We worked quickly to free him, but with no success. The huge jeep was too heavy for us to move. Finally with the aid of the other vehicle and a rope, the jeep was raised so that Dad could pull Grandpa free. As he pulled him from the river to the edge of the road, Dad told us sternly to go up to where the bus was and to wait there.

While the others waited, I silently slipped out to some nearby bushes where I could be alone to talk with Heavenly Father. I prayed for Grandpa's life with all the faith a ten-year-old could muster. I prayed that Heavenly Father would bless him to have a broken leg and nothing else and that he would be all right. I knew that Heavenly Father had heard my prayer and that he wouldn't let me down. It seemed like eternities later when Dad came up to the bus and gathered us around him and softly verified our desperate fears by whispering, "Grandpa is dead."

That statement of Dad's caused my little world to stop working all of a sudden. Why had my prayer been rejected? I couldn't understand.

Following some tears, Dad said, "Come on, kids. Let's go have prayer." We silently walked down to where Grandpa was lying, knelt around him as a family, and Dad led us in prayer.

I shall never forget that moment, seeing Dad reverently crying as he thanked Heavenly Father for Grandpa's life, his great contributions to us, and commended his spirit to the eternities and the great rewards he was worthy of. Dad stood as a giant that day when I needed him so desperately.

Grandpa would no longer bring us presents on Christmas Eve, nor would he ask us if we were scared of him and shake our hands. Heavenly Father had said no to my most earnest prayer when I was sure that he would say yes. How does a ten-year-old boy cope with that type of answer? Where does he go for comfort when he who comforts turns down his urgent request? Towering above the crisis was Dad. Amidst a boy's crumbling world he stood strong and righteous. Firm in faith when our doubts broke loose, there was Dad thanking Father in Heaven for our association with Grandpa and strengthening us.

In times of crisis our Eternal Father has given us our dads to do what he would do if he were here. It is my belief that fathers can serve as an extension of Heavenly Father and that he depends upon us to carry his torch, keeping it lighted for his sons to see in a world sometimes filled with darkness.

Family Welfare Farm

STEPHEN R. COVEY

If all things are spiritual to the Lord, certainly that is true of legitimate efforts to serve one's family. Once when I was serving as a Regional Representative, I was counseling with stake presidents regarding the choice of a regional welfare advisor. We came across a good man, and I asked his stake president about this man's track record on welfare. The president said that it was excellent, that the man understood the program and was very committed to it. But for some reason, he said, the man wouldn't come out on the stake welfare farm on Saturday afternoon with the rest of the brethren. I asked him what the man was doing at that time, and he said sarcastically, "Selling real estate," as if the man was going after filthy lucre and neglecting the work of the kingdom.

I looked the stake president in the eye and said, "President, you mean he's on the family welfare farm. Is that what you mean?"

The president asked, "What are you saying?"

I asked the stake president which would be the more serious kind of apostasy—to neglect the family welfare farm or the stake welfare farm? He thought for a long time and said, "Well, I guess, the family welfare farm."

I said, "Yes, that's correct. 'He that will not provide . . . for his own . . . is worse than an infidel,' as the scripture teaches" (1 Timothy 5:8).

Now, I admit that normally a person can and should do both if he properly organizes and disciplines himself, but we need to be very careful about concluding that stake welfare farm work is work of the kingdom and a person properly taking care of his occupation is secular and self-serving.

The point is that we will never be released from our most important Church job, that of husband and father or wife and mother. It will be with us eternally. We will, however, be released from all of our work on the scaffolding from time to time. Eventually perhaps the scaffolding will be withdrawn and the eternal organization will be the patriarchal family.

The First Steps

Edgar A. Guest

Last night I held my arms to you
And you held yours to mine
And started out to march to me
As any soldier fine.
You lifted up your little feet
And laughingly advanced;
And I stood there and gazed upon
Your first wee steps, entranced.

You gooed and gurgled as you came
Without a sign of fear;
As though you knew, your journey o'er,
I'd greet you with a cheer.
And, what is more, you seemed to know,
Although you are so small,
That I was there, with eager arms,
To save you from a fall.

Three tiny steps you took, and then,
Disaster and dismay!
Your over-confidence had led
Your little feet astray.
You did not see what we could see
Nor fear what us alarms;
You stumbled, but ere you could fall
I caught you in my arms.

You little tyke, in days to come
You'll bravely walk alone,
And you may have to wander paths
Where dangers lurk unknown.

And, Oh, I pray that then, as now,
When accidents befall
You'll still remember that I'm near
To save you from a fall.

"My Mom Knows Everything"

George D. Durrant

When I was in the first grade, school lasted only a half a day for that particular grade. All the other grades went for the full school day. I walked to school with my older brother, and one day when we arrived at the building his friends met us and suggested that we all sluff school that day. At that stage of my development I didn't even know what *sluff* meant. They explained that it meant to go up in the creek bed and play instead of going to school. I didn't know how to read and write very well, but I did know a good idea when I heard it; so I quickly sustained that particular motion and we headed over to the creek bed.

It was a magnificent place to play. The stream was running, we threw into it the bottles that some of the town's men had thoughtfully emptied and left along the banks the night before. As the bottles bobbed up and down on the water, we would throw rocks at them and play as though we were throwing rocks at ships. After we tired of that we'd go and lift up pieces of metal from old wrecked cars nearby. As we did so the lizards would dash out from underneath and we'd chase the lizards and capture them and put them in bottles. Then we'd let them go. I don't think I'd be overrating it to say we had a magnificent experience there that morning.

Finally the others decided it must be almost time for me to go home, because I had to go home at noon, whereas they didn't go home from school until about three o'clock. We had no watches, so my brother and his friends fashioned a sundial; and after some degree of calculation they announced, "It's noon, you'd better head for home."

Taking their word on faith, I made my way toward home. I was approaching the house with a smile on my face when my mother, who was looking through the front window, saw me coming. She came out on the porch to meet me.

"Hi, Mom," I said.

Instead of greeting me as she usually did, she said, "How come you're home a half-hour early?"

"Well, it's after noon, isn't it?"

"No, it's eleven-thirty. How come you're home early?"

I stood there for a few seconds, not knowing what to say. As I looked around I noticed down in the southern sky, in the middle of all the blue, a little white cloud. I decided I'd better think fast, and that's exactly what I did.

"Well, Mom," I said, "see that cloud down there in the sky?"

"Yes," she said.

"The teacher saw it too," I explained. "She thought that might be a storm coming, and she said we'd all better leave school and get home before it started to storm."

From the way my mother looked at me I could tell immediately that she didn't believe me. So I told her the entire truth; I guess I sort of turned "state's evidence." After a severe talking-to (and a spanking that I almost got, but not quite), she asked me to promise never to sluff school again. As I promised her, I thought to myself: "I can't fool her. My mom knows everything. I'd better not ever try anything like that again." And for a long time I didn't.

I found out at that early age that my mom knew some things that were almost outside the scope of human reason. Now, I'll admit it wouldn't have taken a Sherlock Holmes to figure out my particular case of The Boy Who Came Home Early. But there have been other cases in which it was absolutely amazing how my mom seemed to know things that I ought to do and other things that I ought not to do. She could see the whole situation clearly when I couldn't see it at all.

"Congratulations, Dad!"

Matthew Richardson

I guess there are some things in life that, try as you might, you just can't imagine . . . *accurately*. For example, my wife and I had the opportunity to travel to Switzerland. We were excited to see the famed Matterhorn. Whenever I tried to imagine standing at the foot of the Matterhorn, I saw Disneyland. I had visited Disneyland on several occasions, so I knew the Matterhorn (and the bobsled) well. As we rode the train to the tiny town of Zermatt, located at the base of the Matterhorn, my excitement grew. I closed my eyes and imagined Lisa and myself standing at its base. There we were, standing in a field smothered with wild flowers with climbers waving as they walked past to embark on their mountaineering conquest. I even heard the faint bellowing (in stereophonic sound, no less) of the "abominable howl" that I had grown to love/hate in the caverns of the Disney Matterhorn.

Upon our arrival in Zermatt, after a short walk we stood and viewed the Matterhorn. I was taken aback by the beauty. It was so different from what I expected. It was better . . . it was *real*. By the way, there isn't a bobsled ride or abominable snow monster on the *real* Matterhorn (just in case you were wondering).

As happened with the Matterhorn, I have found that my perception of reality often doesn't agree with reality. I remember when my wife first told me she was pregnant. Both she and I were full-time college students, working three jobs between us and struggling to make ends meet. I remember standing in our tiny basement apartment, complete with plumbing for decoration, when my wife broke the news. "I'm pregnant!" she said in excitement. *Pregnant?* my mind questioned. I asked her to call the hospital back and double-check the lab work. "Congratulations, Dad," she said as she hung up the telephone receiver.

Congratulations, Dad? I was excited, but I couldn't get the word *dad* to stop ringing in my ears. *Dad?* My mind raced. Although I looked forward to the experience and even anxiously anticipated it, there was something deep down inside me that was screaming: "You . . . a dad?" How could I possibly be a dad? I didn't even have any power tools! Amidst the mental confusion, there was one comforting thought in the back of my mind: I knew that I had a little time to prepare for the experience. Nine months. At the time, nine months seemed like such a long time. I reasoned that a good contractor can build a house or two in nine months, so surely I could figure out fatherhood in nine months.

Nine *short* months later (it is easy for me, or anyone else who has never been pregnant, to say "nine short months"), I found myself in a situation oddly similar to—yet profoundly different from—the Matterhorn adventure I described earlier. As I stood in a delivery room at the regional medical center, I nervously watched as my wife prepared to deliver our firstborn child. I had viewed the birthing videos, read the pamphlets, and attended the delivery classes at the hospital. I had even memorized all the breathing techniques: panting, "hee-hee-phew," and the final command—"push." I had imagined this day for the past nine months, but my perception of delivery day had not been quite the same as what I was now beholding. This was reality.

I tried to think where those nine *long* months of preparation went. This reminded me of tests I used to take in elementary and secondary school. "This is a test," the proctor would say in a monotone voice. "You have exactly six minutes to finish this section. Pick up your pencils and begin [there was always a long pause]—now!" I would feverishly read, figure, and mark the answers I knew. Then I would go back and guess at the questions I didn't know. After all, the proctor told us that "there is no penalty for guessing." In what seemed more like two minutes than six, the proctor bellowed: "Stop! Time's up. Lay your pencils down." It was unnerving to lay a pencil down when I didn't know all the answers or had been forced to wing it because of the time constraint.

Now I stood in a delivery room with a knot in my stomach and throat, dressed in a flimsy paper suit (complete with booties, mask, and hat that resembled something a far-out painter from France would wear). I could just hear the voice: "Stop! Time's up. You are now a dad." I must admit that reality is often somewhat overwhelming. I couldn't help but recall that well-used cliché, "When the opportunity arises, the time for preparation is past." Since I ran out of time preparing, I supposed I could always guess at or wing fatherhood. As with those timed tests, hopefully there would be no penalty. Yet somehow guessing seemed out of the question. Nine months before, I was certain I would be prepared to be a father, but now my confident statement that "anyone can prepare to be a dad in nine months" came back to haunt me.

What I witnessed in that delivery room was truly a miracle. I was stunned, overwhelmed, overjoyed, and fearful all at once. I honestly never knew I was capable of the depth of feeling I experienced at that time. It was better than I had imagined. This most memorable and striking experience, however, brought everything to a grinding "reality check" when a masked nurse handed me a small, bundled baby boy and said, "Congratulations, Dad!" Déjà vu! My mind raced again. *Dad!?* This time I was actually holding *my* son. How could I be a dad? I *still* didn't have any power tools!

"You Did It Yesterday"

RAND PACKER

For several days I had worked hard shoveling dirt and level-ing our backyard. My bride was delighted that we were at last going to have some turf to mow and romp on. The boys weren't too excited about the new grass, for they had thoroughly enjoyed themselves on and in that quarter acre of dirt. Regardless of the weather the dirt was always dirty, and that's enough to keep any normal boy happy. They took great joy in bringing the dirt into the house, and that's enough to keep any normal mom unhappy. There is an interesting quality about dirt. You can wash it a hun-dred times, and it doesn't get any cleaner.

That evening I rolled the peat moss over the freshly planted seeds, turned on the water, and dreamed of beautiful green shoots soon to appear. The following day I rushed home from work to make sure the watering had been done, and to my anger I discovered three dogs chasing each other on my newly seeded lawn. It looked as if they had just finished a horse race. My fury swelled and I picked up some rocks, shouted some colorful words at the dogs, and threw the rocks at them as hard as I could. I repaired the damaged lawn as best I could and started once again trying to be a model father and husband.

The following day I was relaxing in our big soft chair when I noticed some of the little neighborhood boys coming up the driveway. Suddenly I heard my son who was hiding on the patio yell some distinctly familiar words. Then he started pegging rocks at his little friends, and away they went crying.

I rushed outside, hoping to salvage our family's reputation. "Son, where on earth did you get a notion like that?" I anxiously questioned him. With proud defiance he fired back the answer, "Well, you did it yesterday." I was stunned. His words and actions were a carbon copy of what I had done to the dogs the day before. My, how quick they are to learn, these little giants! And it seems as though negative things are learned more quickly. If my sons were to see me do something like that every day, what a great injustice I was guilty of!

ON THE *Lighter Side*

"*I* Wanted You to Hear Me"

RANDAL A. WRIGHT

I recall a certain new family who moved into our ward: a father and his four little boys. One of the boys was named Issac, a cute little boy with thick glasses and a big cowlick. His parents had been divorced only a few weeks before they moved in. During the Primary's annual sacrament meeting program, I noticed that someone was singing quite loudly. At first I couldn't tell who it was, but soon figured out that it was our new boy, Issac. Before long, all those in attendance had big smiles on their faces as they listened to this young boy sing with all his heart at the top of his lungs. As the program progressed, he became even louder and more expressive. Soon the smiles turned to laughter, as the congregation watched this young man give it everything he had. It was as if he had the solo part and the rest of the Primary children were his backup singers. As the bishop, I was sitting on the stand and could see his father on the back row of the chapel, very red-faced. After the program concluded, Issac's dad made his way toward the stage. I wondered what he would say to his son. When he got to Issac I heard him ask, "Issac, why were you singing so loudly?" The boy replied, "Dad, you were sitting at the back of the church, and I wanted you to hear me sing."

The Little Plumbers

CHRIS CROWE

Every father ought to read the book of Job once in a
while. Why? Because we often need the patience of Job. There
are days—you know what I'm talking about—when if it's not one
thing, it's another. You wake up late, cut yourself shaving, miss
breakfast, and get to work late, a speck of toilet paper still on
your bloody chin. You find out about the important meeting you
were supposed to attend an hour *after* the meeting's over. Your
desk looks like someone detonated a paper bomb on it, and you
spend most of your day trying, in vain, to find the Very Important
Papers you're sure you left there yesterday. The freeway on the
way home moves like the Cougar Stadium parking lot at homecoming. You get home late for the fifth time that week, after you
promised your wife, guaranteed, that you'd be home on time
tonight for sure. And now that you're home, all you want to do is
eat dinner, slink into the living room, and hide behind the newspaper for a while, then go to bed.

But—and you know what I'm talking about if you have
kids—you can't, or don't dare, do that. They need someone to tell
them to turn the TV down, help with homework, provide a ride
to Mutual, cough up money for tomorrow's field trip, referee
squabbles, and, when they're little, provide constant supervision.
Older kids have their own ways of getting into trouble, but it's
usually outside of the home; little ones can make mountains of
headaches right in the privacy of their own home. Those are the
days when you need Job's patience.

I've had my share of such days, but one from several years ago
remains etched in my mind like a kid's handprint on a newly
poured patio. In those days, Christy and Jonathan liked to team up
for fun and mischief while I read the paper and Liz was busy with
dinner. Christy was four, Jonathan was two, so she called the shots.

That evening's shots were called from the bathroom, where the two little plumbers had locked themselves to splash, play, and generally enjoy a little kid's life without any annoying interruptions from Liz or me.

An ominous silence (*all* silences in a house with two kids under five are ominous)—followed by a series of toilet flushes, giggles, and gurgles—alerted Liz and me to the scene. When we crashed their indoor beach party, the kids, the floor, and the walls were drenched with toilet water. Jonathan's yellow bathtub boat bobbed in the gentle tide of the toilet bowl, while the two little culprits, dripping with wide-eyed innocence, tried to explain what had happened.

Liz and I had been in the parenting game long enough not to be fooled by a couple of cherubic looks; the overwhelming circumstantial evidence condemned them on the spot. We disinfected them, spanked them, and sent them outside to safer and drier activities. The evening wore on, as evenings do; the bathroom returned to normal; and we forgot about the incident.

Later that night when I revisited the damp disaster area, it was obvious that somebody (or somebodies) hadn't been flushing the toilet. I didn't think much of it—after all, an unflushed toilet isn't all that unusual in a house inhabited by a four-year-old—and gave the toilet handle a yank.

The tank gurgled, the bowl bubbled, but instead of whirling everything neatly down the toilet drain, the murky water rose over the lip of the bowl, splashed onto the floor and over my bare feet.

I hopped from one foot to the other, yelling for Liz. When she came to the bathroom door, she looked at me sitting on the bathroom counter, my feet dripping wet; at the mess on the floor; and at the steady stream of water spilling over the edge of the toilet bowl.

"Toilet's clogged," she said.

As she stood in the safety of the hallway, I sat on the sink, and together we watched until the water ceased its relentless sludge over the edge of the toilet bowl.

To make a long, grimy story short, the plumber's friend, coat hanger, and Playtex-gloved hand (guess whose hand?) couldn't unplug our toilet again. I knew that on the morrow I would have two unpleasant alternatives: call a plumber and blow a chunk of our savings in one grand flush, or attack the problem myself with screwdriver, wrench, and my bare hands.

I decided to tackle it myself. If it was simple I'd be able to do the job and save the cost of a plumber. If it was complicated, I was sure to make it worse, guaranteeing that the plumber would earn his pay.

That evening around bedtime, as I was contemplating the day's disaster, Christy walked through my room on her way to use *our* toilet. On her way back to her room, I asked her about the day's flooding, hoping to discover what I'd be up against in the next day's amateur plumber hour.

"Christy, 'member when you and Jonathan were playing in the bathroom today?"

She didn't answer. Even a four-year-old knows better than to incriminate herself.

"C'mon," I wheedled, "you're not in trouble now. Do you remember when you two were playing in the toilet?"

She nodded.

"Did you put anything in there besides the boat?"

"Nope," she answered cautiously. "We were just washing it."

"So you didn't put anything else in there? No toys? No dolls? No shoes?"

"No, Daddy. We were just washing the boat."

"Did you use washcloths?"

"Just two."

"Which two?"

"The ones from the hall closet."

"What happened to them?"

"But, Daddy, we were just using 'em to wash the boat . . . one is still okay. I put it back in the closet."

"Still wet?"

"Uh-huh, but I did put it away."

"Great." (Job's patience kicks in about here.) "What about the other?" I asked, anticipating the awful answer.

"It drownded."

"It Tasted Terrible"

Ardeth G. Kapp

One faithful and somewhat idealistic mother reportedly was determined to rid her family of all distracting influences in the home, beginning with negative comments. To put this plan into effect, she announced that the next person who spoke an unkind word would have his or her mouth washed out with soap. Now with any threat, there must be follow-up. In response to the question of whether or not she followed up, she admitted, "Yes, I did, and it tasted terrible."

The Kick Under the Table

EDGAR A. GUEST

After a man has been married awhile,
And his wife has grown used to his manner
     and style,
When she knows from the twinkle that lights
     up his eye
The thoughts he is thinking, the wherefore and
     why,
And just what he'll say, and just what he'll do,
And is sure that he'll make a bad break ere he's
     through,
She has one little trick that she'll work when
     she's able—
She takes a sly kick at him under the table.

He may fancy the story he's telling is true,
Or he's doing the thing which is proper to do;
He may fancy he's holding his own with the
     rest,
The life of the party and right at his best,
When quickly he learns to his utter dismay,
That he mustn't say what he's just started to say.
He is stopped at the place where he hoped to
     begin,
By his wife, who has taken a kick at his shin.

If he picks the wrong fork for the salad, he
     knows
That fact by the feel of his wife's slippered toes.
If he's started a bit of untellable news,
On the calf of his leg there is planted a bruise.
Oh, I wonder sometimes what would happen to
     me

If the wife were not seated just where she
    could be
On guard every minute to watch every trick,
And keep me in line all the time with her kick.

Finger Painting

H. Wallace Goddard

We are more likely to be big when we see as the Father sees, notice and remember the good, understand people's noblest intentions. I think it was just such an understanding that I felt one evening with little Andy. Nancy was away at a meeting, and I was watching the children. While I was washing the dishes, I did not notice the great danger sign familiar to all mothers: the kids were quiet. When I finished the dishes, I entered the family room to find that Andy had discovered the finger paints on the bottom shelf of the bookcase. The bold swatches of brilliant red, yellow, green, and blue were breathtaking on our new carpet. On that occasion I was calm enough to consider: "What does this mean to Andy? Is he trying to torment me? No. Is he merely exploring and enjoying his toddler world? I think so." So I explained to him the advantage of finger painting on slick paper that can be hung on the fridge. "Ohhhhh!" said Andy in a delighted way. And we cleaned up the carpet together.

A Plant for Mom

RANDAL A. WRIGHT

Several years ago our eight-year-old son came in from playing outside, carrying a huge potted plant. He excitedly presented it to his mother as a gift. After thanking him for his thoughtfulness, we asked him where he found this special gift. He told us he'd found it in a clearing behind our home. This just didn't make sense to me. The plant was about five feet tall and very green and healthy. It was obvious that someone had taken good care of it—it was even in a nice container. After further questioning, we had our son show us exactly where he had found the plant. While we couldn't imagine how the plant got there or who had taken such good care of it, we were convinced that our son really found it behind *our* house.

We decided to put the plant in our living room next to the sofa, where it looked very nice. We have frequent visitors to our home, and several people (including our home teachers and several ward and stake leaders) commented on how nice the plant looked in our living room. But something about the plant never seemed right. Maybe it was the strange smell that was always apparent when you sat near it, or the odd feeling we got as we looked at it closely. It looked more like a healthy weed than anything else.

Finally, after about a month, I pulled down a book from the bookshelf to see if I could identify what kind of plant we were tending. I flipped through the pages until I finally spotted a plant that looked exactly like ours. I checked closely to be sure. I even pulled off one of the leaves from our plant and put it on the kitchen stove burner. There was no question about it. We had in our living room a healthy five-foot-tall marijuana plant.

We were so naive! And not only had we harbored the plant in our living room, but we had invited friends and family to sit in its shade!

While my family and I now look back on this experience and laugh, it taught us a sobering lesson that may be useful for all families to consider. We can have inappropriate things in our homes and in our lives and not even recognize the danger. To be safe, we must look closely at our actions and the environment with which we surround ourselves.

"Mama, You've Got Trouble!"

ELAINE CANNON

The tulips squeezed into the little fellow's fist were drooping, and the stems where they had been twisted free from the mother plant were already beginning to string and curl, like dandelion stems we children used to deliberately suck in and blow out on to reshape.

"Mama, you've got trouble!" he said, thrusting the flowers toward her.

It was an appealing sight to this woman so grateful for motherhood, to see her bright little four-year-old and his constant companion of the same age, the neighborhood shepherdess from down the block, standing before her with their spring loot.

"Trouble? Not me," she answered. "I am one happy woman just having you here!" She snuggled the two children to her.

"Hey, Mom, the flowers—you'll mess them up. They're for you." The boy wiggled free and thrust the flowers toward her again. "Well, anyway, Mrs. Bertagnole says for me to tell you that you are in trouble."

"I am in trouble?" The unfamiliar tulips took on new meaning.

"Yes, because I picked all of these flowers. That's what she said. But I did it for you because you said you wanted some tulips, and we don't have any, and Mrs. Bertagnole had these white ones." He breathed a deep sigh and laid the tulips in his mother's lap.

She did have trouble. Why hadn't he gone next door to Troxlers' and picked tulips? the mother wondered. It wouldn't have mattered so much. They had half an acre of bright yellow and multi-striped tulips that had been in the ground many years. But Mrs. Bertagnole really didn't grow flowers. Or children!

"Darling, these are beautiful tulips. But most of all I love you for thinking of me and for coming directly home with them.

Thank you!" And she hugged him again and put her face in the graceful arch of the petals. "I love you for bringing me these beautiful tulips. Now about that trouble we seem to be in. Let's talk it over. First, you forgot to get permission from Mrs. Bertagnole to pick her tulips. Second, why don't we go together to see how we can make her feel better?"

"Mom, I'm glad you are my friend."

ℐources and Permissions

Love

"Gifts of Love" by Ardeth G. Kapp, from *My Neighbor, My Sister, My Friend* (Salt Lake City: Deseret Book Co., 1990), pp. 118–20.

"The Yellow Dress" by Janene Wolsey Baadsgaard, from *Why Does My Mother's Day Potted Plant Always Die?* (Salt Lake City: Deseret Book Co., 1988), pp. ix-xi.

"To This End" by John Oxenham, taken from *Best-Loved Poems of the LDS People* (Deseret Book Co., 1996), pp. 175–76.

"Learning About Love" by Gina Johnson. Previously unpublished.

"'Jeff, I Love You'" by Max H. Molgard, from *Inviting the Spirit into Our Lives* (Salt Lake City: Bookcraft, 1993), pp. 7–8.

"Shards of Good Intentions" by H. Wallace Goddard, from *The Frightful and Joyous Journey of Family Life* (Salt Lake City: Bookcraft, 1997), p. 17.

"Hi, Teacher!" by Sheldon L. Anderson. Previously unpublished.

"The Daily Portion of Love" by H. Burke Peterson, from *A Glimpse of Glory* (Salt Lake City: Bookcraft, 1986), pp. 151–53.

"It Didn't Hurt Anymore" by H. Wallace Goddard, from *The Frightful and Joyous Journey of Family Life* (Salt Lake City: Bookcraft, 1997), p. 83.

Service and Sacrifice

"'Thank You for Letting Me Give to You'" by Harold C. Brown, from "Doing Good and Being Good," in *Every Good Thing: Talks from the 1997 Women's Conference,* ed. Dawn Hall Anderson, Susette Fletcher Green, and Dlora Hall Dalton (Salt Lake City: Deseret Book Co., 1998), p. 93.

" 'Unto One of the Least of These' " by Susan Farr-Fahncke. Previously unpublished.

"Rebel with a 'Claus' " by Gordon Swensen. Previously unpublished.

" 'Where Was He?" ' by H. Burke Peterson, from *A Glimpse of Glory* (Salt Lake City: Bookcraft, 1986), pp. 99–100.

"A Moveable Feast" by Elaine Cannon, from *God Bless the Sick and Afflicted* (Salt Lake City: Bookcraft, 1989), p. 40.

"Those Who Mix the Mortar" by Ardeth G. Kapp, from *My Neighbor, My Sister, My Friend* (Salt Lake City: Deseret Book Co., 1990), p. 101.

"A Bottle of Warm Soda" by Sandra Rogers, from "Stones, Serpents, Swords, Seeds, and Tears," in *Brigham Young University 1993–94 Devotional and Fireside Speeches* (Provo: Brigham Young University, 1994), pp. 182–83.

"The Pure, the Bright, the Beautiful" by Charles Dickens, taken from *Best-Loved Poems of the LDS People* (Salt Lake City: Deseret Book Co., 1996), pp. 114–115.

" 'I Needed to Do a Good Deed' " by Elaine Cannon, from *God Bless the Sick and Afflicted* (Salt Lake City: Bookcraft, 1989), pp. 33–34.

"Carrying On" by Janna DeVore, from *The New Era,* October 1997, pp. 12–15.

The Workings of the Spirit

"She Heard the Blessing" by H. Burke Peterson, from *A Glimpse of Glory* (Salt Lake City: Bookcraft, 1986), pp. 79–81.

"The Recommend" by George D. Durrant, from *Get Ready! Get Called! Go!* (Salt Lake City: Bookcraft, 1979), pp. 16–17.

"Too Busy to Listen" by Harold B. Lee, from *The Teachings of Harold B. Lee,* ed. Clyde J. Williams (Salt Lake City: Bookcraft, 1996), pp. 414–15.

"Listening to the Conscience" by Stephen R. Covey, from *The Divine Center* (Salt Lake City: Bookcraft, 1982), pp. 181–82.

"She Prayed for Whatever She Would Like" by Shirley Thomas, from "Choices and the Holy Ghost," in *To Rejoice as Women: Talks from the 1994 Women's Conference* (Salt Lake City: Deseret Book Co., 1995), pp. 73–74.

"Spirit Letters" by Sheldon L. Anderson. Previously unpublished.

"The Wrestle" by Hugh B. Brown, from *Vision and Valor* (Salt Lake City: Bookcraft, 1971), pp. 237–39.

"Ralph" by Robert E. Wells, from *Hasten My Work* (Salt Lake City: Bookcraft, 1996), pp. 97–99.

"The Radio Analogy" by Harold B. Lee, from *The Teachings of Harold B. Lee,* ed. Clyde J. Williams (Salt Lake City: Bookcraft, 1996), pp. 420–22.

Faith and Prayer

"The Contact Lens" by Richard H. Cracroft, from "Tracing Father's Patterns: 'Taking One Step into the Dark,'" in *My Soul Delighteth in the Scriptures,* ed. H. Wallace Goddard and Richard H. Cracroft (Salt Lake City: Bookcraft, 1999), pp. 37–39.

"Determined to Be Worthy" by H. Burke Peterson, from *A Glimpse of Glory* (Salt Lake City: Bookcraft, 1986), pp. 20–21.

"Strong Son of God" by Alfred, Lord Tennyson, taken from *Best-Loved Poems of the LDS People* (Salt Lake City: Deseret Book Co., 1996), p. 80.

"To Cope with Things I Would Not Choose" by Ardeth G. Kapp, from *My Neighbor, My Sister, My Friend* (Salt Lake City: Deseret Book Co., 1990), pp. 146–51.

"A Generous Employer" by Kevin Stoker, from *Missionary Moments* (Salt Lake City: Bookcraft, 1989), pp. 23–24.

"The Snowstorm" by Randal A. Wright. Previously unpublished.

"More Things Are Wrought by Prayer" by Alfred, Lord Tennyson, taken from *Best-Loved Poems of the LDS People* (Salt Lake City: Deseret Book Co., 1996), p. 269.

"His Eyes Will Be Healed" by Jane D. Brady, in *My Soul Delighteth in the Scriptures,* ed. H. Wallace Goddard and Richard H. Cracroft (Salt Lake City: Bookcraft, 1999), pp. 114–19.

"The Answer Was No" by Anne Osborn Poelman, from *The Simeon Solution* (Salt Lake City: Deseret Book Co., 1995), pp. 93–96.

The Power of the Word

"'A Joy Which Is Unspeakable'" by Neal E. Lambert, from "The Liahona Experience: Getting Directions Through the Scriptures," in *My Soul Delighteth in the Scriptures,* ed. H. Wallace Goddard and Richard H. Cracroft (Salt Lake City: Bookcraft, 1999), pp. 164–66.

"The Time My Father Ripped Up the Book of Mormon" by James H. Fedor. Previously published in *Vigor,* issue 13, December 1996, pp. 1–2.

"Miracles and Family Scripture Study" by Elaine Cannon, from "Experiment on His Word: The Value in Training Up a Child," in *My Soul Delighteth in the Scriptures,* ed. H. Wallace Goddard and Richard H. Cracroft (Salt Lake City: Bookcraft, 1999), pp. 125–27.

"'It's Not a Problem Anymore'" by Brent L. Top. Previously unpublished.

"'Victoria Doesn't Believe'" by Angie T. Hinckley, from "The Covenant to Love and Bear Witness," in *Behold Your Little Ones* (Salt Lake City: Bookcraft, 1999), pp. 28–29.

"A Torn Page" by Robert E. Wells, from *Hasten My Work* (Salt Lake City: Bookcraft, 1996), pp. 24–26.

"'Is This Really Doing Anybody Any Good?'" by Neal E. Lambert, from "The Liahona Experience: Getting Directions Through the Scriptures," in *My Soul Delighteth in the Scriptures,* ed. H. Wallace Goddard and Richard H. Cracroft (Salt Lake City: Bookcraft, 1999), pp. 161–63.

"Lessons Learned in the 'Mole Hole'" by Elaine Cannon, from "Experiment on His Word: The Value in Training Up a Child," in *My Soul Delighteth in the Scriptures,* ed. H. Wallace Goddard and Richard H. Cracroft (Salt Lake City: Bookcraft, 1999), pp. 130–32.

Glimpses of Eternity

" 'The First Game That He Ever Saw Me Play" ' by Sterling W. Sill, from *The Keys of the Kingdom* (Salt Lake City: Bookcraft, 1972), pp. 304–5.

"I Would Give All That I Am" by Melvin J. Ballard, from *Melvin J. Ballard: Crusader for Righteousness* (Salt Lake City: Bookcraft, 1966), pp. 138–39.

"Mirrors of Eternity" by Sheldon L. Anderson. Previously unpublished.

"Higher Authority" by Hugh B. Brown, from *Eternal Quest* (Salt Lake City: Bookcraft, 1956), pp. 221–22.

" 'What Are You Going to Be?' " by Elaine Cannon, from *Life—One to a Customer* (Salt Lake City: Bookcraft, 1981), pp. 115–16.

"Brent" by Bette S. Mogard, from *Everyday Battles* (Salt Lake City: Bookcraft, 1999), pp. 117–19.

"A Glimpse of Heaven" by Royden G. Derrick, from *Temples in the Last Days* (Salt Lake City: Bookcraft, 1987), pp. 145–46.

"I Would Be Worthy" by Hugh B. Brown, from *Eternal Quest* (Salt Lake City: Bookcraft, 1956), p. 13.

" 'Why Haven't You Done My Temple Work?' " by Wendy Bradford Wright, from "Being Friends with Your Ancestors," in *Forever Friends,* ed. Randal A. Wright (Salt Lake City: Bookcraft, 1996), pp. 121–24.

"From God's Point of View" by Bonnie Ballif-Spanvill, from "The Peace Which Passeth Understanding," in *Every Good Thing: Talks From the 1997 Women's Conference,* ed. Dawn Hall Anderson, Susette Fletcher Green, and Dlora Hall Dalton (Salt Lake City: Deseret Book Co., 1998), pp. 129–30.

Missionary Work

"With the Lord's Help" by Hugh B. Brown, from *Eternal Quest* (Salt Lake City: Bookcraft, 1956), pp. 227–32.

" 'Who Has Need of the Physician?' " by Carlos E. Asay, from *The Seven M's of Missionary Service* (Salt Lake City: Bookcraft, 1996), pp. 26–27.

"Salvation's Song" by Sheldon L. Anderson. Previously unpublished.

"An Admonition from a Higher Source" by Orson F. Whitney, from *Through Memory's Halls* (Salt Lake City: Historian's Office, 1930), pp. 81–83.

" 'One Dirty Little Irish Kid' " by Harold B. Lee, from *The Teachings of Harold B. Lee*, ed. Clyde J. Williams (Salt Lake City: Bookcraft, 1996), pp. 602–3.

"They Couldn't Stop Reading" by Kevin Stoker, from *Missionary Moments* (Salt Lake City: Bookcraft, 1989), pp. 125–27.

"The World's Great Heart Is Aching," author unknown, taken from *Best-Loved Poems of the LDS People* (Salt Lake City: Deseret Book Co., 1996), p. 297.

"The Hairdresser" by Robert E. Wells, from *Hasten My Work* (Salt Lake City: Bookcraft, 1996), pp. 16–20.

"Coming Home" by George D. Durrant, from *Get Ready! Get Called! Go!* (Salt Lake City: Bookcraft, 1979), pp. 55–56.

"He Picked 'Mormons' " by Kevin Stoker, from *Missionary Moments* (Salt Lake City: Bookcraft, 1989), pp. 165–68.

Gospel Lessons

"The Former District President" by Robert E. Wells, from *Hasten My Work* (Salt Lake City: Bookcraft, 1996), pp. 59–64.

" 'Why Don't You *Really* Pray About It?' " by H. Burke Peterson, from *A Glimpse of Glory* (Salt Lake City: Bookcraft, 1986), pp. 34–35.

"Where Home Is" by Anne Osborn Poelman, from *The Simeon Solution* (Salt Lake City: Deseret Book Co., 1995), pp. 140–46.

"A Lesson from My Son" by Rand Packer, from *Congratulations: It's a Dad* (Salt Lake City: Bookcraft, 1982), p. 12.

" 'They Never Gave Me My Testimony' " by Stephen R. Covey, from *The Divine Center* (Salt Lake City: Bookcraft, 1982), p. 36.

"The Greater Sin" by Spencer W. Kimball, from *The Miracle of Forgiveness* (Salt Lake City: Bookcraft, 1969), pp. 281–82.

"My Priorities" by Bette S. Molgard, from *Everyday Battles* (Salt Lake City: Bookcraft, 1999), pp. 59–61.

" 'Tell Me How You Do It' " by Hugh B. Brown, from *Eternal Quest* (Salt Lake City: Bookcraft, 1956), pp. 196–200.

"Unity or Uniformity?" by Anne Osborn Poelman, from *The Simeon Solution* (Salt Lake City: Deseret Book Co., 1995), pp. 122–28.

Character and Attitude

"Putting Character Above Popularity" by Jeanette Hales Beckham, from "Lessons That Have Helped Me," in *Brigham Young University 1992–93 Devotional and Fireside Speeches* (Provo: Brigham Young University, 1993), pp. 86–87.

" 'She Became an Angel' " by Stephen R. Covey, from *The Divine Center* (Salt Lake City: Bookcraft, 1982), pp. 25–28.

"The Parable of the Treasure-Vault" by James E. Talmage, from *The Improvement Era* 17(October 1914): pp. 1108–9.

"Heroes" by Edgar A. Guest, from *Just Folks* (Chicago: Reilly & Lee Co., 1917), pp. 68–69.

" 'Make It a Good Day!' " by Elaine Cannon, from *Life—One to a Customer* (Salt Lake City: Bookcraft, 1981), pp. 11–12.

"The Positives Approach" by Joseph L. Bishop, from *The Making of a Missionary* (Salt Lake City: Bookcraft, 1982), pp. 53–56.

"Soccer Practice" by Marilynne Todd Linford, from *A Woman Fulfilled* (Salt Lake City: Bookcraft, 1992), pp. 5–6.

"Climbing Mt. Olympus" by George D. Durrant, from *My Best Day So Far* (Salt Lake City: Bookcraft, 1990), pp. 11–17.

" 'I Can't Sing This' " by Randal A. Wright. Previously unpublished.

"He Would Not Give In" by Joseph L. Bishop, from *The Making of a Missionary* (Salt Lake City: Bookcraft, 1982), pp. 59–60.

"The Roller-Skating Incident" by Matthew Richardson, from *Fathering* (Salt Lake City: Bookcraft, 1996), pp. 65–67.

Home and Family

"A Kiss from Dad" by George D. Durrant, from *The Art of Raising Parents: A Young Person's Guide* (Salt Lake City: Bookcraft, 1977), pp. 49–51.

"Only a Dad" by Edgar A. Guest, from *A Heap O' Livin'* (Chicago: Reilly & Britton Co., 1916), p. 42.

" 'Don't Forget, Mom' " by Karen J. Ashton, from "Happiness Intended," in *Behold Your Little Ones,* ed. Barbara B. Smith and Shirley W. Thomas (Salt Lake City: Bookcraft, 1999), pp. 66–67.

"Grandpa" by Rand Packer, from *Congratulations: It's a Dad* (Salt Lake City: Bookcraft, 1982), pp. 18–20.

"Family Welfare Farm" by Stephen R. Covey, from *The Divine Center* (Salt Lake City: Bookcraft, 1982), pp. 122–23.

"The First Steps" by Edgar A. Guest, from *Just Folks* (Chicago: Reilly & Lee Co., 1917), pp. 85–86.

" 'My Mom Knows Everything' " by George D. Durrant, from *The Art of Raising Parents: A Young Person's Guide* (Salt Lake City: Bookcraft, 1977), pp. 79–81.

"'Congratulations, Dad!'" by Matthew Richardson, from *Fathering* (Salt Lake City: Bookcraft, 1996), pp. 1–4.

"'You Did It Yesterday'" by Rand Packer, from *Congratulations: It's a Dad* (Salt Lake City: Bookcraft, 1982), pp. 21–22.

On the Lighter Side

"'I Wanted You to Hear Me'" by Randal A. Wright. Previously unpublished.

"The Little Plumbers" by Chris Crowe, from *Fatherhood, Football, and Turning Forty* (Salt Lake City: Bookcraft, 1995), pp. 39–42.

"'It Tasted Terrible'" by Ardeth G. Kapp, from *My Neighbor, My Sister, My Friend* (Salt Lake City: Deseret Book Co., 1990), p. 101.

"The Kick Under the Table" by Edgar A. Guest, from *When Day Is Done* (Chicago: Reilly & Lee Co., 1921), pp. 105–6.

"Finger Painting" by H. Wallace Goddard, from *The Frightful and Joyous Journey of Family Life* (Salt Lake City: Bookcraft, 1997), pp. 70–71.

"A Plant for Mom" by Randal A. Wright. Previously unpublished.

"'Mama, You've Got Trouble!'" by Elaine Cannon, from *God Bless the Sick and Afflicted* (Salt Lake City: Bookcraft, 1989), pp. 19–20.